Blessings In Disguise

Unveiling the Hidden Gifts in Life's Challenges

Deb Lamperd

Copyright © 2024 Deb Lamperd

All rights reserved. No part of this book may be used or reproduced by any means, graphic, electronic or mechanical, including photocopying, recording, taping or by any information storage retrieval system without the written permission of the publisher and copyright holder; except in the case of brief quotations embodied in critical articles and reviews:

:

DEDICATION

For mum. 1938 - 2024
For Tania, Sam and Bill .. my blessings in disguise

INDEX

Introduction ... 1

Blessing 1*: Good Luck, Bad Luck, Who Knows   4

Blessing 2*: Perfect Imperfection   8

Blessing 3*: Can You Forgive?   11

Blessing 4*: Embracing Emptiness   15

Blessing 5*: Words Have Consequences   18

Blessing 6*: A Child's Heart   21

Blessing 7*: Noticing Synchronicities   26

Blessing 8*: Happiness is Within   29

Blessing 9*: Change Your Mind   33

Blessing 10*: One Bad Day   36

Blessing 11*: Handling Life's Disappointments   39

Blessing 12*: Dare to Be Different   44

Blessing 13*: Cultivating Curiosity   47

Blessing 14*: Dancing to Nature's Song   50

Blessing 15*: Judge Me Not   55

Blessing 16*: Your Time to Shine   58

Blessing 17*: In Search of the Magical Other   61

Blessing 18*: Abracadabra- "I Create As I Speak"   66

Blessing 19*: It Ends With You   69

Blessing 20*: The Glory of a Friendship   72

Blessing 21*: Face Your Fear   77

Blessing 22*: The Road Less Travelled   80

Blessing 23*: The Boldness of Commitment   83

Blessing 24*: The Game of Life   88

Blessing 25*: Winners and Losers   91

Blessing 26*: What's Your Motive?   94

Blessing 27*: The Spiritual Power of Gratitude   98

Blessing 28*: Embracing Transformation   102

Blessing 29*: The Secret   105

Blessing 30*: Entering "The Arena"   110

Recommended Reading:

Introduction

Welcome to the threshold of a transformative journey, a portal into the realm of *"Blessings in Disguise."* As you turn these pages, allow yourself to entertain the possibility that the universe, in its infinite wisdom, has orchestrated the arrival of this book into your hands at precisely this moment in your life. It is an invitation, a gentle nudge from the cosmos, to guide you back to the profound remembrance of your true spiritual essence and purpose.

"Blessings in Disguise" is not merely a book; it is a sanctuary of revelations borne of my own pilgrimage through the landscapes of the soul, a journey that found its genesis on January 7th, 2008. This pivotal day marked the end of an 18-year marriage, heralding the onset of a profound personal upheaval characterized by PTSD, depression, and bi-polar disorder. The ensuing five years became a passage through the shadows, necessitating the guidance of both psychiatrists and psychologists as I endeavoured to navigate the uncharted territories of this newfound existence.

My background as a police officer of 26 years, with its reservoir of suppressed traumas, compounded the complexity of this transformation. Additionally, the mantle of motherhood—to two boys, then aged 12 and 10—cast its own unique light and shadows upon the path, intensifying the emotional landscape of this period of change.

It was in this crucible of transformation that the poems within this book were conceived—whispers of the soul captured in moments of solitude and communion with the universe. These verses flowed forth in the quiet hours before dawn, under the canopy of the night sky, as I sought solace and understanding in the silent dialogue with the cosmos. *"Blessings in Disguise,"* the poem that lent its name to this compilation, emerged as a beacon of hope, a reassurance that, despite the tumult, all would be well.

Encouraged by my sister-in-law, I initially shared these insights and poems on a Facebook page of the same name, where they resonated with a community of souls navigating their own spiritual journeys. The entries in this book are both a reflection of those initial musings and a testament to the evolution of my spiritual understanding. They are reshaped and expanded to echo the growth of my soul's voice over the intervening years, incorporating both the original insights and new revelations that speak to the breadth of my spiritual journey.

Life, in its relentless march, continued to sculpt my spirit through trials and tribulations, from the loss of my home and the transient nature of rental living to the physical ordeal of ulcerative colitis, which found relief through acupuncture after six long years. The transition to medical retirement after more than a quarter-century in police service, the ebb and flow of friendships, the specter of homelessness, and the poignant loss of my mother to cancer—all these experiences have woven the rich, complex tapestry of my existence.

I share these facets of my journey not from a pedestal of unchallenged tranquility but from the trenches of lived experience, from the heart of someone who has walked through the fire and emerged transformed. The blessings and poems within these pages are the distillation of wisdom gleaned from the crucible of life's challenges, reflections of the spiritual awakening that has been both my companion and my healer.

It is with a spirit of profound humility and hope that I extend these insights to you, dear reader. May they serve as lanterns on your path, illuminating the way through the darker passages of your own journey. May they remind you that within every challenge lies the seed of a blessing, waiting to be discovered. Through the prism of these pages, I invite you to view your own experiences through a lens of transformation and grace, to embrace the alchemy of the soul that transmutes pain into wisdom, and to find, nestled within the folds of life's trials, your own blessings in disguise.

Blessing *1.   Good Luck, Bad Luck, Who Knows

In the labyrinth of life's experiences, Eastern philosophy offers a profound paradox that challenges our conventional perceptions of fortune and misfortune, encapsulated in the adage, "*Good luck, bad luck, who knows?*" This concept, emblematic of the yin and yang, serves as a reminder of the intricate balance that governs our existence, where within every adversity lies the seed of a blessing, and within every blessing, the shadow of potential adversity. It underscores the fluid nature of life's circumstances, suggesting that the essence of our experiences is not fixed but ever-changing, colored by the perspectives we choose to adopt.

William Shakespeare, in his timeless wisdom, mirrors this sentiment in "*As You Like It*," illustrating how adversity, though venomous and ugly like the toad, can bear precious jewels. He writes:

> "Sweet are the uses of adversity, which, like the toad, ugly and venomous, wears yet a precious jewel in his head; and this our life, exempt from public haunt, finds tongues in trees, books in the running brooks, sermons in stones, and good in every thing."

Shakespeare invites us to find beauty and value in the trials we endure, proposing that adversity is not merely an obstacle to be overcome but a teacher, a guide that leads us to uncover the profundity and richness embedded in the fabric of life. This perspective echoes the Eastern understanding of duality, where every aspect of existence is interwoven with its opposite, each giving meaning and context to the other.

The yin and yang symbol, a representation of this fundamental duality, encapsulates the harmony of opposites, demonstrating how light and darkness, joy and sorrow, success and failure are intrinsically connected. It teaches us that life's experiences are not to be categorized simplistically as good or bad but to be embraced in their totality, recognizing the potential for growth and enlightenment inherent in every moment. This symbol serves as a visual testament to the balance that permeates the universe, reminding us that the flow of life encompasses all, moving in cycles and seasons, each with its lessons and gifts.

At the heart of this philosophy lies the understanding that our attitude towards life's unfolding drama plays a pivotal role in shaping our experience of it. When faced with challenges, our perception determines whether we see them as insurmountable obstacles or opportunities for growth. Similarly, in moments of victory, our attitude dictates whether we remain humble and open to the lessons of success or become ensnared by the trappings of achievement. It is our mindset, our chosen frame of reference, that imbues our experiences with meaning, transforming the mundane into the miraculous, the painful into the powerful. Viktor Frankl, a holocaust survivor, and author of *"Man's Search for Meaning"* wrote of this ability to choose one's attitude:

> "Everything can be taken from a man but one thing: the last of the human freedoms—to choose one's attitude in any given set of circumstances, to choose one's own way."

The wisdom of "*good luck, bad luck, who knows?*" encourages a stance of openness, curiosity, and non-attachment towards life's vicissitudes. It invites us to relinquish our tight grip on expectations and outcomes, to flow with the currents of change with grace and flexibility. By adopting this perspective, we learn to appreciate the transient nature of all things, finding peace in the understanding that both joy and sorrow are but temporary visitors in the grand scheme of our existence. As the ancient Persian adage reminds us; *"this too shall pass."*

This approach to life cultivates a deep sense of resilience and equanimity, enabling us to navigate the highs and lows with a steady heart and a clear mind. It teaches us to extract wisdom from every experience, to see the hidden blessings in adversity, and to remain vigilant to the lessons cloaked in success. In doing so, we align ourselves with the fundamental truths of the universe, embracing the dance of duality with open arms and a courageous heart.

Moreover, this philosophy offers a pathway to compassion and empathy, as we recognize that just as we are subject to the ebb and flow of fortune, so too are those around us. It fosters a sense of connectedness, a realization that we are all participants in this shared journey of life, each with our own battles and triumphs, each with our own stories of resilience and transformation.

In the embrace of "good luck, bad luck, who knows?" we find a powerful antidote to the rigidity of judgment and the pain of resistance. We learn to meet life with a sense of wonder and acceptance, to find serenity in the face of uncertainty, and to trust in the unfolding of our journey, knowing that within every moment lies the potential for growth, learning, and transcendence.

Thus, as we traverse the varied landscape of our lives, let us carry with us the wisdom of the East and the insight of Shakespeare, finding tongues in trees, books in running brooks, sermons in stones, and good in everything. Let us remember that the true measure of our fortune lies not in the external circumstances we encounter but in the quality of our response to them, in our ability to discern harmony, grace, and purpose in the fabric of life.

"Blessings in Disguise"

She hides her face in darkness and calls upon the light,
to find you in your darkest hour, weakened by the fight.
Her hand out stretched to lift you up from down on bended knee.
A stranger or a friend, not known, her face you cannot see.

Life's journey takes you on its ride, where fear and sorrow have its place,
At times so overwhelming, you doubt God's loving grace.
Hold the faith that she will find you, be certain she'll arrive.
There is no soul upon this earth, whose heart she will deprive.

The call goes out from wounded hearts, filled with such despair.
To send to you an angels love, in answer to your prayer.
Look behind the loss you mourn, into the empty space,
for there you'll find her blessings stand right there in its place.

She brings to you the strength within to rise again with each new day.
To start afresh, a second chance, to meet all trials that come your way.
What she knows is not revealed, until the perfect time.
That blessing in your fate awaits, together they're entwined.

From the dust of fallen stars, new dreams arise from deep within.
Her hand in yours, inspires you on, to try life once again,
Be filled with love and faith, that she sends from God to you.
Never doubt one single day your dreams will all come true.

Look deep within the eyes of that soul you greet today.
Listen oh so carefully to what they do or say.
For behind the mask they wear, you may well be surprised,
The person that you least expect, is your blessing in disguise.

Blessing *2. Perfect Imperfection

Spun within the complex web of life, interwoven with innumerable aspirations, desires, and dreams, there lies a persistent and often elusive quest for perfection. This pursuit, deeply ingrained from the earliest moments of our existence, shadows our every step, whispering promises of fulfillment that remain just beyond reach. As I once penned in a poem, *"Do not seek from me perfection because I'll surely let you down,"* there lies an acknowledgment of our inherent fallibility and the futility of chasing an ideal that, by its nature, is unattainable.

From the initial cry that announces our arrival into the world to the final whisper of our departure, society imposes upon us a standard of perfection that seems not only daunting but fundamentally at odds with the essence of our being. Through academic achievements, professional milestones, and even the accolades that celebrate our supposed superiority, we are taught to value ourselves and others through the lens of this unrelenting expectation. Yet, beneath this veneer of achievement and recognition lies a more insidious effect—the internalization of a belief that our worth is contingent upon meeting these external benchmarks of success.

Nowhere is this quest for perfection more poignant and damaging than in the realm of our closest relationships. In seeking flawlessness from those we hold dear—a partner, friend, sibling, or even the divine—we unwittingly set the stage for disappointment and disillusionment. This relentless scrutiny, this measurement of worth against an idealized standard, can lead us to overlook the beauty of the imperfect bonds that make our lives rich and meaningful.

This same relentless pursuit extends its reach into every corner of our lives, from the ceaseless striving for a more beautiful home to the dissatisfaction that taints our professional endeavours and travel experiences. The pervasive culture of critique and comparison, fuelled by ratings and reviews, perpetuates a cycle of discontent and complaining, forever chasing a mirage of perfection that dances just out of grasp.

Yet, as the years gather and the pursuit wearies, a profound realization dawns—that the standard of perfection we sought was a chimera, an illusion that led us away from the very essence of life's beauty. The question then arises: Who deemed perfection the pinnacle of achievement? Who decided that it was the standard by which all should be measured?

In the serene beauty of Japanese culture, influenced by the deep wells of Buddhist philosophy, we find the concept of *wabi-sabi*—a celebration of the beauty found in impermanence, imperfection, and incompleteness. This ancient wisdom, a quiet yet powerful rebellion against the tyranny of perfection, offers a lens through which to view the universe not in spite of its flaws but because of them. Wabi-sabi invites us to embrace the paradox that it is the imperfection of the cosmos that renders it truly perfect.

What, then, can wabi-sabi teach the West about relinquishing the unyielding grip of perfectionism? How can this philosophy guide us to a place of acceptance and appreciation for the beauty inherent in the flawed and the unfinished?

By adopting the principles of wabi-sabi, we learn to view our relationships and our lives through a lens of compassion and understanding. We begin to see the cracks and rough edges not as blemishes to be corrected but as marks of character and authenticity. In this shift of perception, we discover the freedom to love without condition, to appreciate the unique beauty of each moment and each being, without the distortion of impossible standards.

This journey towards embracing imperfection is not merely an aesthetic choice but a profound spiritual awakening. It is an acknowledgment that the essence of life, in all its messy and glorious reality, is a canvas of constant evolution, never complete, never perfect, but always beautiful in its impermanence.

As we navigate the path of life, let us carry with us the wisdom of wabi-sabi, allowing it to illuminate the richness of the imperfect, the transient, and the incomplete. In doing so, we open our hearts to the true perfection that lies in acceptance, in the recognition of our shared humanity, and in the celebration of the divinely flawed tapestry of existence.

Let "Perfect Imperfection" be our mantra, a guiding light towards a life lived in full colour, unafraid of the shadows, and enriched by the very imperfections that make us beautifully human. In this embrace of the imperfect, we find not only peace but a deeper, more authentic connection to ourselves, to others, and to the universe itself.

Blessing *3.   Can You Forgive?

Do you remember those quaint desk calendars we used to have that would show a daily quote of wisdom before the digital versions took their place? The essence of wisdom they shared remains timeless. One such pearl was, *"to err is human, to forgive is divine,"* This quote resonates deeply in the current era, compelling us to reflect on its profound simplicity and enduring truth.

In the realm of human experience, the motif of forgiveness weaves through the narrative of virtually every life story. Among the myriad forms it takes, self-forgiveness stands out as a pivotal chapter. How many of us, ensnared by the shadows of past mistakes, replay them incessantly, as if our minds were stuck on a loop, unable to break free from a haunting refrain? The seductive whisper of ego convinces us there's value in nursing our grievances, in holding on to pain as though it were a piece of our identity. But at what cost?

The burden of unresolved past actions is akin to a digital screenshot of shame and guilt, meticulously archived in the recesses of our minds, awaiting some future moment of reckoning. This self-imposed sentence of carrying forward our guilt serves no purpose but to anchor us to a stagnant version of ourselves. Forgiveness, then, emerges as a powerful act of liberation—a means to hit the 'delete' button on these snapshots of self-reproach, making room for the creation of new, unburdened narratives.

Forgiveness is not about erasing history or absolving ourselves or others of responsibility; rather, it's about extracting the wisdom from our experiences and allowing the rest to dissolve. It's a process of renewal, a refresh button for the soul, enabling us to step into new possibilities unshackled by the past.

Our present moment is a furnace for creation, a point from which we sculpt our future. The emotional and physical states we inhabit are not just passive experiences but active ingredients in the reality we manifest. Clinging to past sorrows and regrets is like feeding an addiction, one that injects a steady stream of toxic chemicals into our bodies with every recollection. This cycle of emotional turmoil can manifest physically, reinforcing the connection between mind, body, and spirit. To break free is to acknowledge that our health and well-being are inextricably linked to the thoughts we nurture and the past we choose to release.

Life, in its infinite complexity, offers us the freedom to choose. We can cling to past wounds, wrapping them around us like a well-worn sweater, or we can choose to let go, to forgive ourselves, and to move forward. Perhaps those old calendar quotes, like the one about forgiveness, were not just quaint reminders but beacons of wisdom for those willing to see. To forgive is to bestow upon oneself a divine gift—the freedom to live unencumbered by the past and open to the infinite possibilities of now.

In today's world, where change is the only constant, and the pace of life seems ever-accelerating, the act of forgiveness is more relevant than ever. It is a testament to our capacity for growth, compassion, and transformation. As we negotiate the complexities of modern day life, let us remember that forgiveness is not just an act of divine grace but a vital, life-affirming choice we can make every day. It is an invitation to release ourselves from the chains of the past and embrace the limitless potential of the present. So, why not accept this gift?

"Forgiveness is Divine"

As you sit in quiet reflection at the end of every day.
You may contemplate what happened, how things turned out this way.
Your heart may ache inside with a memory that is blue.
A handprint on your heart that's left reminds you all was true.

"To err is only human", the scriptures share that truth to heal.
To seek from every lesson that pearl of wisdom to reveal.
To live within a world, to be left so unforgiven.
Calls on strength before unknown, to simply keep on living.

Not known another's burden, the weight of cross they bear.
Inside your heart be grateful, it's not their shoes you wear.
For those that seek from you, a heart that does forgive.
It's your chance to grant the gift of grace, that only you can give.

To say that "I forgive you" can just be words so hollow.
The gift is not the spoken word, but what you do that follows.
To live it every day, within your heart so true.
Then the gift you give to them is also one for you.

As we tarry through a lifetime, our regrets may be but few.
For it's not those things we did that count, but those we did not do.
There may well be a reason for those cards we're dealt to play.
A chance to see what Ace you keep and those you give away.

In your heart is found the strength to live with what you've done.
To find your own forgiveness, where before there was but none.
The past it is released, it was never meant to stay.
You take from it the lessons learnt and send it on its way.

Look deep within your heart and soul and see if there is hidden,
No act or deed dealt to you that cannot be forgiven.

May you find the courage and the strength hidden in this line,
"To err is only human, but forgiveness is divine."

Blessing *4. Embracing Emptiness

Within the vast fabric of life, where each strand crafts the story of our experiences, there lies a profound, often overlooked wisdom in the art of embracing emptiness, of allowing voids to exist on the diary pages of our daily routines. The ancient philosopher Aristotle introduced the concept of *"horror vacui,"* the idea that nature abhors a vacuum, suggesting that the universe instinctively seeks to fill any emptiness with new forms of being and matter. This universal principle, observable in the natural world, extends its influence into the intricacies of human life, where voids, be they physical spaces or temporal gaps, seldom remain unfilled.

This phenomenon, mirrored in the rush to occupy a vacated position, the rapid transformation of landscapes, or the swift rebound from lost relationships, reveals a deeper, often unexamined impulse within us—a resistance to emptiness and a relentless pursuit to maintain a state of perpetual fullness. The modern ethos, with its sanctification of busyness, embodies this resistance, championing a lifestyle where every moment is accounted for, every silence filled with noise, and every gap in our schedules packed with activity.

Yet, what if this incessant compulsion to fill the voids of our lives runs counter to a more profound, spiritual law of the universe? What if, in our dogged avoidance of emptiness, we inadvertently close off channels through which growth, renewal, and creativity might flow?

Eastern philosophies, through practices such as mindfulness and meditation, invite us to explore the transformative potential of the void. They teach us the value of becoming an *"empty cup,"* of cultivating a space within the mind where silence reigns, and preconceptions vanish. This state of mental emptiness, far from being a lack, is envisioned as a fertile ground for spiritual nourishment, a realm of pure potential where the seeds of our deepest growth can germinate.

By embracing a mindset of indifference—not in the sense of apathy but as an open receptivity devoid of rigid expectations—we align ourselves with the divine mind, the state of pure awareness, or Being. This alignment is not a passive resignation but a dynamic state of presence, a readiness to receive whatever the universe deems necessary for our soul's journey toward enlightenment.

In this sacred emptiness, we discover that the universe operates not through the imposition of our will but through the graceful orchestration of circumstances and encounters that resonate with our deepest needs for spiritual evolution. It is here, in the void, that we become attuned to the subtle movements of the cosmos, to the ebb and flow of creation that guides us gently toward our destiny.

The wisdom of "*God's rejection is God's protection*" and the concept of a "*Blessing in Disguise*" gain new depth within this context. They remind us that what we perceive as absence, loss, or denial may, in fact, be the universe's way of redirecting us toward paths of greater fulfillment and purpose. Not getting what we want becomes not a denial of our desires but an invitation to explore desires we never knew we had, leading us to discover joys and fulfillments beyond our imagination.

This radical approach to life, though seemingly antithetical to the ethos of Western cultures, offers a gateway to a more profound understanding of existence. By consciously creating voids in our lives, by allowing spaces of uncertainty to dwell within our days, we open ourselves to the magic of the universe. This magic is not the conjuring of material possessions or superficial achievements but the deeper alchemy of the soul's transformation.

To live gracefully with uncertainty, to welcome the void with open arms, is to dance with the universe in a partnership of co-creation. It is to acknowledge that in the space of emptiness, in the cradle of silence, lies the potential for infinite creation, for the manifestation of our true spiritual essence.

As we journey through life, let us dare to leave empty spaces in our canvas, to relish the beauty of the unscripted and the unplanned. Let us cultivate a comfortable abode for uncertainty, for it is in the embrace of the unknown that we discover not only who we truly are but also who we are destined to become. In this sacred space of emptiness, we find not absence but presence, not lack but abundance, and not fear but love, guiding us ever onward in our quest for spiritual awakening and fulfillment.

Blessing *5. Words Have Consequences

Within the complex dynamics of human interactions and relationships, the power of words stands as a potent force, capable of shaping destinies in ways beyond our immediate comprehension. This truth is starkly illustrated in a story that intertwines the realms of psychological experimentation, personal conviction, and societal impact, bringing to light the profound consequences our words and actions can have on the lives of others, sometimes unfolding in ways we could never predict or intend.

The tale begins in the early years of the Cold War, a period marked by paranoia and espionage, where psychologist Henry Murray embarked on a project aimed at unraveling the human psyche to better understand and manipulate it. Within the hallowed halls of Harvard University, under the guise of Project MKUltra, Murray initiated an experiment that would leave an indelible mark on one participant, a young student who, for the purposes of the study, was dubbed "Lawful."

Lawful was subjected to a harrowing ordeal, designed to test the limits of his psyche. Tasked with writing an essay expressing his core beliefs for what was promised to be a benign debate, he instead faced a brutal interrogation. His values, the very essence of his identity, were mercilessly dissected and derided by an aggressive inquisitor. This relentless scrutiny did not elicit the expected defensive reaction; instead, it fractured the young man's sense of self, propelling him into a state of disarray.

The psychological scars from this ordeal lingered, leading him to renounce his academic achievements and retreat into solitude in the wilderness. However, the embers of his conviction, rather than being extinguished, were slowly fanned into a blaze. Over the years,

Lawful painstakingly refined his essay, his beliefs crystallizing into a manifesto he deemed so vital that he resorted to extreme measures to disseminate his message. The result was "Industrial Society and its Future," better known to the world as The Unabomber Manifesto.

This story is a stark reminder of the weight our words carry and the unforeseeable paths they can chart in the lives of others. Lawful's transformation from a university mathematics prodigy to the Unabomber, driven by the conviction that his ideas could either save or doom society, underscores the unpredictable power of influence. It demonstrates how a single experience, especially one as emotionally charged and demeaning as the one he endured, can alter the trajectory of a life in profound and tragic ways.

The spiritual lesson woven through this narrative speaks to the heart of our interconnectedness and the responsibility that comes with it. It calls us to recognize that every action, every word, holds the potential to echo far beyond its intended reach, crafting ripples that touch lives and shape realities in ways we may never witness. This understanding impels us towards a path of mindfulness, urging us to tread lightly and compassionately in our interactions with others, aware of the latent power we wield.

Moreover, the story invites reflection on the nature of belief and conviction. It challenges us to consider the sources of our deepest convictions and the manner in which we choose to express and act upon them. In a world where words can be both a balm and a blade, the tale of Lawful serves as a cautionary parable on the ethics of influence and the sanctity of the individual psyche.

In grappling with the aftermath of our deeds and words, we are faced with the task of bearing witness to the garments woven from our actions. This witnessing is not a passive act but a sacred responsibility, a call to live with intentionality and grace, mindful of the indelible marks we leave as a legacy of our existence.

As we navigate the complexities of human interaction and the moral landscapes of our times, let us do so with a deep awareness of the impact of our words and actions. May we strive to be architects of healing and understanding, wielding the power of our words as instruments of compassion and agents of positive change. In this conscious engagement with the world and those who inhabit it, we find the path to a more mindful, empathetic, and interconnected existence, where the echoes of our influence resonate with the harmony of understanding and mutual respect.

Blessing *6. A Child's Heart

In the sanctum of our hearts, where the divine love for a child dwells, there lies a profound responsibility—a duty not merely to wish for their happiness and health but to recognize the inevitable journey through life's intricate weave of trials and triumphs. This sacred charge asks of us to be the guardians of their growth, understanding that the path of life spares no one from adversity, yet it is precisely through these challenges that the soul is sculpted and wisdom birthed.

Spiritual teachings illuminate the truth that our most enduring lessons are not gleaned from the words of others or the pages of a book, but through the crucible of our experiences. Each incarnation, a unique opportunity for spiritual evolution, brings with it the promise of growth, often most profoundly realized in moments of strife. As stewards of a child's heart, our gaze upon our own life's mosaic of joy and sorrow offers the invaluable insight that it is not the absence of adversity that defines our journey, but the resilience and grace with which we navigate it. As Lilly Andaman writes in her novel, *"The Well: Revealing the Hidden Nature of Reality:"*

> "Maybe then, as parents, when asked what do we aspire for our children, a new answer could be contemplated. Instead of seeking to protect them from hardships and adversities, rather we nurture them towards one of resilience. When we come to understand the challenges of life as leading us towards a greater opportunity to unveil the enigma and mystery of our inner truth, to reach the pinnacles of self-realisation, then those challenges are transformed into an adventure rather than one of pain and suffering. Adversities reveal opportunities to reclaim our inherent birth rite, that being an understanding of the intrinsic unity of all life and our eternal

and infinite connection to the Divine Creator." p.204

To prepare a child for the undulating journey ahead is to imbue them with resilience, to equip them with the inner strength to rise from the ashes of defeat, and to glean the hidden wisdom nestled within every trial. Our legacy is not measured by the shields we craft to guard them from the slings and arrows of fate, but by the fortitude they display in facing them, transforming potential scars into badges of honor and growth.

Among the most precious gifts we can bestow upon a child is the treasure of self-esteem, a compass by which they can navigate life's storms. It is our solemn duty to plant and nurture the seeds of belief in their inherent worth and potential, fostering a deep-rooted sense of self that will be their lantern in the darkest nights. This journey towards self-love and acknowledgment is an odyssey in its own right, one that begins anew with each soul's arrival into this world.

Kahlil Gibran, in his timeless wisdom, offers a beacon of guidance: *"You may strive to be like them, but seek not to make them like you."* These words serve as a gentle reminder to cherish and cultivate the nascent dreams within a child's heart, to refrain from imposing our unfulfilled desires upon their shoulders. Every soul comes with its own melody to contribute to the symphony of existence, its path lit by the flames of passion and enthusiasm. To divert a child from their innate calling is to dim this light, replacing it with a void of yearning, a sense of something essential missing from their essence.

Our society bears witness to the consequences of such diversion, as countless individuals seek to fill the voids within through myriad forms of addiction, a testament to the unaddressed yearnings of the heart. Gibran's metaphor of the parent as the bow and the child as the arrow poignantly encapsulates our role: to aim with love and then let go, allowing the child to soar towards their destiny, propelled by the force of our belief and love.

Embracing this sacred duty, we understand that the ultimate gift we can offer is not to hold them tethered to our dreams but to empower them to unfold their wings, to fly towards their own horizon with the strength and conviction we've helped instill. This act of letting go, though fraught with uncertainty, is an act of profound love and trust in the journey of the soul.

As custodians of a child's heart, our task is monumental yet imbued with beauty. We are called to be both teacher and student, guardian and guide, as we walk alongside them, bearing witness to the unfolding of their unique journey. In this sacred dance, we learn the art of unconditional love, of support without constraint, celebrating each step, each leap, with joy and reverence.

The journey of nurturing a child's heart is a mirror to our own spiritual path, reflecting the lessons of love, resilience, and the eternal cycle of growth and renewal. It invites us to examine our own hearts, to heal our wounds, and to embrace our vulnerabilities, for in doing so, we model the courage and authenticity we wish to instill in them.

In the realm of spirituality, where the heart's wisdom transcends the spoken word, we find the strength and grace to guide the young souls entrusted to our care. Together, we discover that the journey of life, with all its vicissitudes, is not a tale of seeking fulfillment outside ourselves but a pilgrimage towards the light within, a light that guides us back to our own divine essence and interconnectedness with all life.

Thus, in the loving embrace of a child's heart, we find not only our greatest responsibility but our most profound calling—to nurture, guide, and ultimately release them into the world, arrows soaring towards their destiny, leaving trails of light in their wake.

"Bright Eyes"

*I gazed into my newborn's eyes and wondered what I'd done,
to deserve a gift as grand as this, the treasure of my son.
Through many years and sleepless nights I watched him start to bloom,
like a butterfly spreads its wings when leaving its cocoon.*

*I was there when he did walk, and then I watched him run,
" Look how fast I go" he said "come and watch me Mum. "
I kissed away his tears and bathed his wounded knees,
I read his favorite stories of pirates sailing Seven Seas.*

*The trees that he did climb got bigger every year,
the courage in his heart did grow, at times he had no fear.
"One day I'll climb a mountain mum so I can play with snow."
"Yes," I said, "I'm sure you will, now off to school you go."*

*The brightest light shines within, when I look into his eyes.
The dreams inside my young child's heart reflect his soul's desires.
At play he is an astronaut who flies up to the moon,
watching Earth, far below, in the safety of his room.*

*Through the passing of the years I watched my son become a man;
now he waits beside the door with suitcase in his hand.
His eyes still shine so bright like many years ago,
those dreams inside, now set free, to nurture and to grow.*

*As I hold him to my heart, I said, "I love you son,"
" Live your life with love and honour, for no deed can be undone."
"Sew the seeds of your respect to those souls that you will meet."
"Those blessings will return to you, for what you so you sew you reap.*

"Go and climb your mountain and scale the highest peak,"
"life is in adventure, revealed in goals you seek."
"Inspire those around you with what you say and do,"
"Your greatest gift lies within, to yourself be true. "

As I watched him walk away, a tear from me did seep.
I knew inside, that gift of mine, was never one to keep.
A child is just the future, hidden in disguise,
their dreams revealed, for all to see, in the brightness of their eyes.

Blessing *7.   Noticing Synchronicities

In the intricate dance of existence, the concept of synchronicity emerges as a profound illumination, revealing the interconnectedness of all things, not through the lens of random coincidence, but as the manifestation of a divine orchestration. This realization transcends the mere acknowledgment of serendipitous encounters, inviting us to perceive each moment, each meeting, as imbued with purpose and significance. Deepak Chopra, in his insightful exploration "*SynchroDestiny*," delves into the spiritual and scientific dimensions of synchronicity, offering a window into the mechanics by which the Universal Spirit molds the fabric of reality through intent.

Synchronicity, as Chopra elucidates, is not merely a source of amusement or bewildering chance but a beacon guiding us towards alignment with our deeper purpose and the intentions of the Universal Spirit. This alignment, a harmonious confluence of our personal desires with the evolutionary impulse of the cosmos, paves the way for a life rich in meaningful coincidences and profound realizations. The principle at the heart of this phenomenon is the recognition that our intentions, when woven with the threads of the greater good, invite synchronistic events that propel us along our destined path.

The underlying science of synchronicity, grounded in the principle that intent transforms spirit into material form, unveils the dynamic interplay between the local self (our individual consciousness) and the non-local (the universal consciousness). This interaction suggests that intentions capable of serving both personal fulfillment and the collective evolution are met with the supportive current of synchronistic occurrences. It is within this sacred partnership that the potential for genuine joy, fulfillment, and transformative impact is realized.

Chopra's insights beckon us to pay heed to the coincidences that punctuate our lives, to inquire into their significance, and to discern the messages woven into their occurrence. By attuning our awareness to these synchronistic events, we become participants in a co-creative process, where our focused attention and openness to guidance amplify the frequency and clarity of such moments, unveiling the path laid out by the Universal Spirit.

The wisdom encapsulated in the Serenity Prayer, attributed to theologian Richard Niebuhr, resonates deeply with the essence of synchronicity. It acknowledges the discernment required to navigate the voyage of life, recognizing what lies within our power to change and what we must gracefully accept. This wisdom, when applied to our understanding of synchronicity, illuminates the delicate balance between action and surrender, between shaping our destiny and yielding to the flow of a higher will.

Synchronicity, then, serves as a compass, pointing towards our alignment or resistance to the Universal Spirit's greater energy. It is in this alignment that the doorways to the realization of our dreams and the fulfillment of our purpose swing wide open, where the seeming coincidences of our lives are understood as threads in the larger tapestry of a divine plan. Within this framework, every encounter, every seemingly random event, is charged with potential and meaning, guiding us towards our ultimate destiny.

As we navigate the journey of life, armed with the knowledge and acceptance of synchronicity, we are invited to surrender to the flow of universal energy, to trust in the unfolding of a plan far greater than our individual desires. This surrender does not diminish our agency but enhances our ability to co-create with the cosmos, to live in harmonious alignment with the evolutionary impulse that guides all of existence.

In embracing synchronicity, we open ourselves to the infinite possibilities that arise from this divine collaboration. We learn to see the world not as a series of isolated incidents but as a web of interconnectedness, where every moment is ripe with opportunity and every coincidence a message from the cosmos. This perspective transforms our understanding of reality, empowering us to live with greater intention, clarity, and connection to the universal forces that animate our world.

Thus, the journey into the heart of synchronicity is not just an exploration of spiritual or scientific curiosity but a profound return to the essence of who we are and the purpose we are here to fulfill. It is a reminder that we are not mere spectators in the drama of existence but active participants in a cosmic dance, where every step, every turn, is guided by the hand of synchronicity, leading us towards the realization of our deepest desires and the actualization of our highest selves.

Blessing *8. Happiness is Within

Embracing happiness is akin to rediscovering a divine state of being, a luminous realm where we are in perfect harmony with our true essence. This joyful alignment is our natural state, the home of our inner being, making any detour into unhappiness feel like an arduous journey away from our authentic self. It is in these moments of disconnection that we hear the call, a gentle nudge to return to the innate joy that resides within us, as natural and as vital as the air we breathe.

Having navigated the tumultuous waters of depression, I have come to treasure happiness not just as an emotional state but as a sacred quest, an eternal journey towards the light that guides us through the darkest of times. Spirituality, in its boundless wisdom, acts as a compass on this quest, illuminating the path to true happiness. Across the vast landscapes of spiritual literature, a resonant theme emerges: the search for happiness in externalities—in people, places, and events—is a pursuit doomed to lead us away from joy and into the clutches of suffering.

This pursuit places upon our shoulders the heavy burden of expectation, the belief that happiness can be bestowed upon us by the world outside. Yet, as the profound teachings of Buddhism remind us, happiness is a flower that blooms from within, its roots deep in the soil of our soul, untouched by the external world's whims. *"Happiness comes from within, and it cannot be found by making the world conform to your desires,"* the sages tell us, guiding us back to the power that lies in our own hands.

Ralph Waldo Emerson, in his timeless wisdom, questions the rationale behind outsourcing our happiness, challenging us to reclaim our joy: *"Why should my happiness depend upon the thoughts in someone else's head?"* he proclaimed. This inquiry beckons us to a radical realization—that happiness is an innate capability, a self-generated miracle of our being. Psychologist and author, Dan Gilbert, in his book *"Stumbling on Happiness"* suggests through the concept of "*synthesized happiness,*" introduces us to our psychological immune system, our inbuilt alchemy that transmutes any situation, transforming our perspective to foster well-being irrespective of external circumstances.

Buddhist philosophy, with its principles of non-attachment and non-judgement, reveals the keys to liberation from suffering and discontent. Our experiences of pleasure and pain are intricately tied to the tapestry of our expectations and perceptions. The chasm between "*what we expect*" and "*what is*" becomes the breeding ground for dissatisfaction. Yet, it is within our power to bridge this gap, to alter our perceptions and, in doing so, to cultivate our own garden of happiness, independent of the changing landscapes around us.

Cognitive Behaviour Therapy, is modern psychology's approach to depression and anxiety, echoes this ancient wisdom. It reinforces the transformative potential of positive self-talk and thoughts, underscoring our capacity to navigate our way back to health and harmony through the power of our mind.

Rudolf Steiner, in his philosophical explorations, reminds us that our direct engagement with the world through thinking and perceiving shapes our reality. Buddhism's profound assertion that everything "*Is as It is,*" devoid of inherent good or bad, invites us to a dance of perception where our thoughts alone paint the colors of our world. This realization places the reins of happiness firmly in our hands, empowering us to cultivate joy irrespective of life's external storms.

The mastery of happiness, then, becomes not just an act of personal fulfillment but a powerful magnet, attracting into our lives those people, places, and circumstances that resonate with our inner state of joy. The Law of Attraction assures us that this alignment is not merely wishful thinking but a universal principle, as inevitable as the dawn.

As we awaken each day to the adventure of life, let us set forth on our quest for happiness with intention and zeal. Let every thought, every action, be a step towards generating the radiance of joy, and watch as the universe, in its infinite grace, mirrors back to us a reality filled with miracles and wonders. For in the embrace of happiness, we find not only our greatest ally but also the key to unlocking the full majesty and potential of our amazing life.

"Colours of the Rainbow"

Like a painting on a wall that calls on gazing eyes to rest a while on me,
To see each stroke of color the artists hand has magically set free.
The canvas used was blank and bare at the very start,
Now it comes alive, a story painted from the heart.

Let me gaze into your eyes like that painting on the wall,
Are you Picasso or a Rembrandt, or just a crayon scrawl?
Have you used the colors of the rainbow, so colorful and bright?
Or seen your life so simple and just used black and white

Does the sun shine on your canvas with children playing there?
Or just have clouds of darkness that reflect your deep despair.
Is the sea you draw so calm and blue, where rivers flow to meet?
Or maybe you have crashing waves that knock you off your feet.

Do your eyes reflect a portrait of every soul who has given you their heart?
Where love has guided the artist's hand to your finest piece of art.
Does the face you see smile back at you to reflect the joy that life has been?
Or one where eyes are closed, to block out tragedies you've seen.

Do you paint mountains high with snowfall on the highest peak?
Are those mountains a reflection of the challenges of life each day you seek.
Or are there rolling hills that meander as far as the eye can see,
that change their colours with the season and see all that life can be.

Give to me the palette in your heart that holds all the colors of the rainbow.
The one I hold is black and white that reflects the life I know.
Guide my hand to paint a life using all the colours that you see,
so I, in turn, can gaze upon the colours that others see in me.

Blessing *9. Change Your Mind

Albert Einstein, a titan of intellect whose insights revolutionized our understanding of the universe, posited a simple yet profound notion:

> "The world that we have made as a result of the level of thinking we have done thus far creates problems that we cannot solve at the same level as the level we created them at."

This statement beckons us to explore the depths of consciousness, beyond the surface-level awareness that navigates our daily existence. Consciousness, as Einstein alluded to, is not merely the state of being awake versus asleep, but a complex, mysterious facet of our reality that transcends habitual thought patterns.

The realm of Universal Mind, or what might be termed as Infinite Intelligence, presents a vast sea of potential that underlies everything in existence. This isn't a concept reserved for the musings of spiritual enthusiasts or New Age thinkers; rather, it finds grounding in the empirical realm of Quantum Physics. The discipline itself delves into the interconnectedness of all things, a web of existence where each thread is entwined with the next, revealing a tapestry of cosmic intelligence and consciousness.

The annals of scientific discovery are replete with instances where monumental insights emerged not from routine mental processes but from moments of profound connection to this Universal Mind. The legendary apple that purportedly inspired Newton's theories on gravity, and Einstein's own Theory of Relativity, envisioned in a dream, stand as testaments to the power of transcending conventional thought to tap into a higher order of understanding.

Moreover, the extraordinary capabilities of autistic savants, including unparalleled memory(hyperthymesia), mathematical prowess, and musical genius and prodigies, further challenge our conventional views on the source of intelligence and creativity. These phenomena, inexplicable through the lens of ordinary human cognition, hint at a deeper, more universal source of knowledge and insight. The 19th century inventor and genius Nikola Tesla was once quoted as saying:

> "The gift of mental power comes from God, divine being, and if we concentrate our minds on that truth, we become in tune with this great power."

This brings us to a pivotal realization: the belief in our limitations is a grand delusion. The notion that we must tirelessly ruminate over our problems, ensnared in worry and stress, is a misconception that undermines our well-being. Such a perspective anchors us to the ego, a limited aspect of our consciousness responsible for creating the very dilemmas we seek to escape.

The truth is, access to the Universal Mind is not an exclusive privilege of savants and geniuses; it is a birthright, inherent to our very existence. The key lies in shifting our approach to problem-solving—moving from a state of constant deliberation to one of release and trust in the flow of insight and inspiration. By envisioning our challenges as already resolved, by stepping back and allowing our minds to wander, to relax, we open the doors to the universe's infinite wisdom.

This shift in mindset, from worry to wonder, from stress to serenity, is not just a philosophical exercise but a practical approach to unlocking our full potential. It's an invitation to view life through a lens of simplicity, recognizing that the complexity often lies not in the challenges themselves but in our reactions to them. By embracing a stance of letting go, we align ourselves with the universe's language, one that speaks in solutions rather than problems, in insights rather than obstacles.

The journey to tapping into the Universal Mind begins with a single step: a decision to change our way of thinking. It's a process of unlearning the patterns that bind us to the mundane and relearning the art of intuition and inspiration. As we embark on this path, we discover that the solutions to our problems have always been within reach, waiting for us to clear the mental clutter that obscures them.

Einstein's insight serves as a beacon, guiding us towards a deeper understanding of ourselves and our place in the cosmos. It challenges us to transcend the limitations of our ego-driven thought processes and to embrace a more expansive, interconnected mode of consciousness. In doing so, we not only solve the problems at hand but also unlock a wellspring of creativity, innovation, and understanding that can transform our lives and the world around us.

In essence, changing our minds is about more than just adopting a new way of thinking; it's about awakening to the vast potential that resides within us, tapping into the universal currents that connect us all. It's a realization that our greatest resources—insight, creativity, wisdom—are not merely human attributes but universal gifts, accessible to all who seek them.

As we venture into this exploration of consciousness and its impact on reality, we open ourselves to a world of possibilities where the boundaries between the individual and the universal blur. In this space, problems become portals to greater understanding, and the act of letting go becomes an act of powerful creation. The journey of changing our minds is thus not just a personal endeavor but a cosmic adventure, inviting us to participate in the unfolding of a more enlightened, interconnected reality. (If you would like to explore this subject in more depth I highly recommend *"The Well: Revealing the Hidden Nature of Reality"* by Lilly Andaman.)

Blessing *10. One Bad Day

Wisdom often surfaces from the most unexpected sources, illuminating truths about our shared human experience. One such revelation comes from an unlikely philosopher, the Joker, in the narrative of "*The Killing Joke*" within the Batman universe. His words, "*All it takes is one bad day*," echoes a profound truth about the fragility and unpredictability of our existence. This sentiment captures the essence of our collective vulnerability — the idea that the line between stability and chaos is as thin as a thread, and that thread can snap with the weight of a single, unforeseen event.

Life, in its boundless complexity, operates not on the linear and predictable pathways we often wish it to but moves in rhythms and cycles, punctuated by moments of calm and tempest. It is within this dance of constancy and upheaval that we find ourselves walking the tightrope of routine, immersed in the comfortable familiarity of our daily patterns, akin to the perpetual recurrence of "Groundhog Day." Yet, the universe, in its infinite wisdom and caprice, occasionally redirects our course with the force of a gale, thrusting us into the depths of uncertainty with events that challenge the very foundations of our reality.

Such moments of disruption — be it through a sudden loss, an unexpected departure, or a life-altering revelation — serve as poignant reminders of our shared susceptibility to fate's whims. The plunge from the mundane into the turmoil of change is a journey that any one of us may be compelled to undertake at any given moment, without warning, without choice.

This understanding brings to light the importance of withholding judgment towards those we encounter who are navigating the aftermath of their own "bad day." Society, with its quickness to judge and categorize, often overlooks the intricate web of circumstances that lead individuals to their present state. There exists a tendency to attribute one's misfortunes to personal failings — poor decisions, a lack of effort, or naivety — casting judgment from a perceived moral high ground, without fully grasping the unpredictability and impartiality of life's challenges.

The teachings of Buddhism offer a counter-narrative to this inclination, advocating for compassion as a guiding principle in our interactions with others. Compassion invites us to recognize the universality of suffering and the potential for any one of us to find ourselves in the throes of adversity. It calls us to empathize with the plight of another, to understand that the ground beneath our feet is as susceptible to shifting as it is for anyone else.

Embracing compassion means to look beyond the surface of someone's circumstances, to see the person before the situation, and to ask ourselves how we might wish to be treated were we in their shoes. It is about extending a hand, offering support, or simply acknowledging their existence with kindness and understanding. It is in these moments of genuine connection and empathy that we not only alleviate the burdens of others but also enrich our own souls, fostering a deeper sense of community and shared humanity.

The capacity to change perspective, to place ourselves in the heart of another's experience, is one of the most transformative powers we possess. It allows us to transcend the barriers of ego and judgment, to touch the essence of another's being with grace and love. This shift in viewpoint not only illuminates the path to personal growth and spiritual awakening but also weaves a stronger, more compassionate fabric of society.

As we navigate the unpredictable waters of existence, let us carry with us the wisdom that "*all it takes is one bad day*" to alter the course of a life. Let this understanding be a beacon of compassion, guiding our interactions and judgments. May we remember that beneath the veneer of circumstance lies a shared vulnerability, a common thread that binds us all in the human experience.

In cultivating a heart of compassion, we open ourselves to the beauty of connection, to the power of empathy, and to the infinite potential for kindness that resides within us. Through this lens, we see not the other but a reflection of ourselves, a reminder of our own fragility, strength, and capacity for change. In this recognition lies the key to a more understanding, forgiving, and united world, where the trials of one are met with the support of many, and where every soul, regardless of its journey, is seen, valued, and loved.

Blessing *11. Handling Life's Disappointments

As we traverse the path of life, we often carry with us the weight of promises unfulfilled, dreams that seem to dissolve before our very eyes, and the lingering sensation of disenchantment. From our earliest days, we are fed tales of a world where hard work, education, and perseverance are the keys to unlocking doors of success, love, and happiness. We grow, nurturing the belief in a fairy-tale ending, convinced that life owes us our "*happily ever after.*" Yet, what do we do when these promises feel like echoes in a void, when the life we encounter starkly contrasts the one we were led to expect?

This pervasive feeling of being ripped off or short changed by life, of standing on the shores of existence and watching as the waves of disappointment wash over our dreams, is a crucible within which profound spiritual lessons are hidden, waiting to be unveiled. It is in the grappling with life's apparent injustices that we are invited to delve deeper into our inner motives, to question, and ultimately to transcend the narratives we have been handed by our societies culture and programming.

The disillusionment, the sense of betrayal by the very principles we were taught to hold sacred, serves as a potent catalyst for spiritual awakening. It beckons us to question not the fairness of life but the nature of the promises we were made. Were they truly guarantees of happiness and fulfillment, or were they signposts pointing us towards a deeper understanding of joy and success, one not measured by external achievements but by internal peace and resilience?

This juncture, where disillusionment meets introspection, is where the spiritual journey takes a profound turn. The realization that life is not a series of transactions, where effort is directly proportional to reward, frees us from the shackles of expectation. It opens our eyes to the beauty of uncertainty, to the richness of experience that lies beyond the narrow confines of societal definitions of success and happiness.

The spiritual lesson embedded within the heartache of unmet expectations is one of surrender, not to defeat, but to the flow of life itself. It teaches us to release our grip on the need for life to unfold in a predetermined manner, to embrace the unpredictable nature of existence with openness and grace. This surrender is not an act of resignation but a declaration of freedom from the tyranny of expectations. It allows us to live fully in the present, to find joy in the journey rather than fixating on the destination.

Moreover, life's disappointments invite us to redefine our understanding of happiness and success, to discover that true contentment arises not from acquiring or achieving but from a deep sense of connection to ourselves, to others, and to the world around us. They teach us that happiness is not a state to be pursued but a byproduct of living authentically, of aligning our actions with our deepest values and truths.

In the face of life's unfulfilled promises, we are called to cultivate resilience, to find strength in vulnerability, and wisdom in the recognition of our own impermanence. This awareness propels us towards compassion, both for ourselves and for others, as we recognize the shared nature of our struggles and aspirations.

The spiritual awakening that emerges from the ashes of disillusionment is a rebirth, a shedding of illusions in favor of a more grounded and expansive perspective on life. It is a journey towards wholeness, where the fragments of broken dreams become the seeds of a more profound understanding of joy, one that is inclusive of pain, growth, and the beauty of the impermanent.

As we navigate the twists and turns of this journey, let us hold space for our disappointments, knowing that within them lie hidden gifts of insight and transformation. Let us weave a new narrative, one that honors the complexity of the human experience, celebrating our capacity to find light in the darkness, to extract meaning from the chaos.

In this reimagining of our story, we discover that the true promise of life is not in the fulfillment of youthful dreams but in the richness of the journey itself, in the depth of our connections, and in the resilience of the human spirit. This understanding does not diminish the pain of disillusionment but transforms it into a portal to deeper wisdom and compassion.

Life, in all its unpredictability and imperfection, invites us to dance to the rhythm of its unfolding, to find grace in the face of disappointment, and to trust in the journey, even when the destination remains shrouded in mystery. In this dance, we are not diminished by our challenges but are elevated by our response to them, crafting a life that is not defined by what we have achieved or acquired but by who we have become in the process.

Thus, in the tapestry of our existence, every thread of disappointment is interwoven with potential for growth, every shattered expectation a window to a more profound understanding of joy. It is in the unweaving of life's illusions that we discover the true beauty of our journey, a beauty marked not by the absence of hardship but by our resilience in the face of it, by our capacity to transform adversity into insight, and by our unwavering commitment to uncover the lessons veiled within each challenge. This process of unweaving the illusions—of peeling back the layers of our preconceived notions and expectations—reveals the essence of who we are and who we can become. It is a journey that calls us to embrace the full spectrum of our human experience, recognizing that the path to enlightenment is not paved with unbroken happiness, but with the wisdom gleaned from the depths of our trials and tribulations. Through this transformative process, we come to see that true beauty and joy are not destinations to be reached, but treasures to be uncovered within the very fabric of our lives, shining forth in moments of grace, love, and connection.

"Broken Dreams"

I looked upon my broken dreams lying at my feet,
an aching heart, deep inside, the tears from me did seep.
"Where's my happy ending Lord?" "Wasn't that the deal?"
Everything familiar, gone, there's nothing now that's real.

So many dreams, in my mind, of a life lived well.
Adventures, deeds and destiny, so many tales to tell.
I promised you, I'd do my best, seeds of kindness I would sow.
In return, all I asked, was love for me bestow.

So take from me my broken dreams, I give them all to you.
Put them back together, I've seen what power of Grace can do.
I'm not going nowhere, I'll wait here till it's done.
So hurry up, get started, from my list take number one.

I hung around and waited, my life I put on hold.
I learnt to be so patient, for my miracle to unfold.
From dawn to dusk, a month, a year, the time did soldier on.
"Come on Lord, tell me now, what's taking you so long?"

The Lord replied, "My loving child, what was I to do?"
"Those dreams were old, from years gone by, so many you outgrew."
"I had prepared for you these new ones, more fitting of your size."
"But, your back you turned, refused to look, with blinkers on your eyes!"

I turned around and stared in awe at new dreams standing there.
I could not believe the wasted years, not seen these gifts so rare.
"Thank you Lord for showing me, to release those dreams of past."
Instead, I'm free, each day to see, new dreams for me you cast.

Blessing *12.   Dare to Be Different

In the intricate dance of existence, where the rhythm is often dictated by the silent yet potent forces of social convention and conformity, lies a profound inquiry into the essence of our being. How much of our lives, one might wonder, are navigated by the unseen currents of collective norms and habits? These conventions, these unwritten codes that govern behavior, act as invisible molds, shaping the matrix of a society, ensuring harmony and uniformity. Yet, within this harmony, there lurks a paradox—a subtle yet persistent pressure that demands conformity at the cost of individual authenticity and creativity.

At the heart of this societal paradox is the herd mentality, a phenomenon that champions sameness and vilifies divergence. To step away from the collective direction is to risk becoming an outlier, subject to the harsh scrutiny of judgment, ridicule, and, in more extreme cases, social ostracism. This mechanism, designed to preserve the status quo, raises a fundamental question about the nature of human judgment and the dichotomy between our celebration of innovation and our resistance to difference.

The celebration of genius—the artist, the inventor, the visionary—reveals society's deep-seated appreciation for creativity and the courage to think differently. These individuals, with their unparalleled contributions, infuse society with vibrancy, innovation, and progress. Yet, ironically, the same society that lauds the extraordinary often shuns those who, in other aspects of being, deviate from the norm.

This contradiction underscores a critical truth: conventions are not innate truths but learned behaviors. The realization that our perceptions are shaped by our cultural milieu opens the door to a world of possibilities. It invites us to question, to explore, and to embrace the diversity of human experience that extends far beyond the confines of our immediate environment. In the vast diversity of global cultures, what is deemed acceptable or taboo varies immensely, reminding us that right and wrong are often matters of consensus rather than universal absolutes.

The journey towards understanding and acceptance begins with the ancient wisdom of *"walking a mile in another man's moccasins."* This exercise in empathy challenges us to confront our prejudices by imagining life through the lens of those we might judge. What if the circumstances of our birth, our appearance, or our abilities were different? Such contemplation not only humanizes those we might have dismissed but also illuminates the richness of experiences that lie beyond the superficial judgments that divide us.

The spiritual journey, then, emerges as a lighthouse of hope, a light that leads away from the shadows of conformity and towards the light of authentic self-expression. It is a call to rediscover the unique essence that each of us carries, to celebrate our individuality, and to contribute our unique voice to the chorus of humanity. This journey is not a rejection of society but an invitation to enrich it, to weave new patterns of understanding and connection that honor the diversity of human expression.

In this context, the act of thinking for oneself becomes an act of rebellion and liberation. It is a deliberate choice to break free from the chains of conventional thinking and to explore the vast landscape of ideas, beliefs, and perspectives that make up the human experience. This choice, though fraught with challenges, is also filled with the promise of growth, creativity, and deeper connection.

Imagine a world where differences are not merely tolerated but celebrated, where the curiosity to understand the other replaces the haste to judge, and where every individual is encouraged to shine in their authentic brilliance. This world is not a utopian fantasy but a potential reality that begins with each of us. It starts with the courage to question, to learn, and to open our hearts to the myriad ways of being that exist.

As we embark on this spiritual voyage, let us hold curiosity as our compass and empathy as our guide. Let us challenge the conventions that limit us and embrace the boundless creativity and potential that define us. In doing so, we not only liberate ourselves but also pave the way for a society that thrives on authenticity, diversity, and genuine connection.

The game of life, reimagined through the lens of individuality and spiritual awakening, becomes not a path of conformity but a journey of discovery. It is a journey that celebrates the unique contributions of each traveler, recognizing that within the mosaic of human experience, every piece is essential, every story valuable, and every soul a repository of infinite potential. In this reenvisioned world, the true measure of success is not adherence to social norms but the courage to live as one's truest self, radiating authenticity and inspiring others to do the same.

Blessing *13. Cultivating Curiosity

In the vast expanse of the human experience, our perceptions are often shrouded in the veils of judgment, obscuring the limitless horizons that lie beyond our conditioned viewpoints. This proclivity to judge, to categorize the world into neatly defined boxes of right and wrong, black and white, us and them, serves as a formidable barrier to the spiritual seeker's quest for enlightenment. Our judgments, born of ingrained beliefs and unexamined convictions, not only limit our understanding of the multifaceted nature of reality but also tether our spirits to a realm of duality, far removed from the unity and diversity that truly define existence.

The spiritual journey, at its core, is an odyssey of perception, a pilgrimage towards the dissolution of these barriers that constrain our vision and impede our growth. It beckons us to cleanse the lens through which we view the world, to embrace the full spectrum of life with all its hues, shades, and variations. This path to clarity and expanded awareness is illuminated by a singular, transformative attitude: curiosity.

Cultivating curiosity is an act of liberation, a deliberate choice to venture beyond the limitations of judgment into a realm of open exploration and wonder. It is an invitation to question, to explore, and to seek understanding in place of condemnation. Curiosity propels us out of the comfort zones of our preconceived notions and into the rich, uncharted territories of new ideas, perspectives, and possibilities.

By adopting an attitude of curiosity, we relinquish the need for certainty and control that underlies our judgments. We allow ourselves to be vulnerable, to admit that we do not have all the answers, and that perhaps, the answers we do have might benefit from reexamination. This humility is the first step towards genuine wisdom, for it acknowledges the infinite complexity of the universe and our place within it as seekers, learners, and explorers.

Curiosity, therefore, becomes a sacred tool in the spiritual seeker's arsenal, a key that unlocks the doors to deeper understanding and connection. It encourages us to look beyond the surface, to delve into the heart of matters with an open mind and a compassionate heart. In doing so, we discover that the world is not a fixed entity, defined by immutable laws of black and white, but a dynamic, ever-evolving tapestry of experiences, each offering unique lessons and insights.

This shift from judgment to curiosity also fosters a profound sense of unity and empathy. As we begin to explore the world from a place of genuine interest and openness, we recognize the common threads that bind us to one another and to all of existence. We see that our differences, rather than being reasons for division, are opportunities for learning and growth. We come to understand that every person, every situation, holds within it a universe of possibilities, waiting to be discovered and appreciated.

Moreover, curiosity rekindles the sense of wonder and awe that is often lost in adulthood. It invites us to see the world with the fresh eyes of a child, to marvel at the beauty and mystery that surround us every day. This renewed sense of wonder not only enriches our lives but also deepens our spiritual practice, reminding us that the divine can be found in the most ordinary of moments and the simplest of things.

Cultivating an attitude of curiosity is, ultimately, an act of profound spiritual significance. It signifies a willingness to embark on a journey of endless discovery, to continually expand the boundaries of our understanding, and to embrace the infinite diversity of the cosmos with love and reverence. It is a commitment to live not in the shadows of judgment but in the light of exploration and acceptance.

As we navigate the path of spiritual awakening, let us embrace curiosity as our guiding light, our compass pointing towards the unbounded realms of knowledge, connection, and truth. In doing so, we not only transcend the limitations imposed by judgment but also open ourselves to a more fulfilling, enlightened existence. In the garden of the spirit, curiosity is the water that nourishes, the sun that illuminates, and the soil from which the flowers of wisdom and compassion bloom.

Blessing *14.   Dancing to Natures Song

In the grand performance of existence, each of us plays a unique part in nature's splendid orchestra, our lives interwoven with the rhythmic cycles that dictate the ebb and flow of all things. Observing nature teaches us invaluable lessons on living in harmony and peace, revealing the universal law of cycles that governs every form of life, from the microscopic to the macrocosmic.

This law serves as a reminder that change is not only inevitable but also integral to the fabric of existence, manifesting in its own time and manner. Life itself unfolds as a perpetual cycle of endings and beginnings, presenting us with the choice to either align with the flow of life or resist its natural course. This decision shapes much of our contentment or dissatisfaction, as Eastern philosophies and spiritual teachings advocate for a posture of allowance and surrender, embracing the wisdom that everything occurs for a reason.

Epictetus, the ancient Greek philosopher, encapsulates this ethos by urging us to desire that everything unfolds precisely as it does, highlighting the power of acceptance:

> "Learn to wish that everything should come to pass exactly as it does."

Similarly, Dan Millman in *"The Laws of the Spirit"* elucidates the significance of timing in our actions and thoughts, suggesting that aligning our endeavors with the rising and falling energies can lead to ease and fulfillment in our pursuits: He writes:

> "All things have a favourable and least favourable time, doors open and doors close, energies rise and fall. A thought or action initiated while energy is rising and growing momentum travels along easily towards completion. But

> some thoughts on a descending cycle have a reduced impact. ..... there is wisdom to know when to act and when to keep still." p.85

Astrology and numerology offer tools for navigating our alignment with the universe's energies, empowering us to seize opportunities and cultivate patience and faith when necessary. Faith, as Marianne Williamson describes in "*A Return to Love*," is the trust that the universe is conspiring in our favor, guiding us towards an ever-unfolding good:

> "Faith is believing that the Universe is on our side, and that the Universe knows what it is doing. Faith is a psychology and awareness of an unfolding force for good constantly at work in all dimensions. Our attempt to direct this force only interferes with it. Our willingness to relax into it allows it to work on our behalf." p.52

This perspective encourages us to relinquish the need to control life's direction, instead inviting us to trust in the universe's wisdom and benevolence.

Adversity, when viewed through the lens of cyclical energy, gains a new dimension, reminding us that life's challenges are often precursors to periods of growth and elevation. It teaches us the value of gratitude and appreciation, especially during our lowest ebbs, which often harbor the seeds of profound personal transformation. Likewise, moments of joy and happiness are to be cherished as transient guests, celebrated for their presence but acknowledged for their impermanence.

Living in awareness of the cycles that surround us fosters a deep-seated faith and trust in the universal love that aims for our greater good. Nature itself, in its unbounded beauty and complexity, stands as a testament to this truth, offering constant evidence of the universe's loving embrace. Carol S. Pearson, in "*Consider the Butterfly*," beautifully articulates this sentiment:

> "I know only as much of God and the world as a creature with two eyes must. But what I do understand, I love, and what I don't understand, I trust." p.10

This blend of love and trust forms the foundation for a life lived in harmony with the universe's rhythms, a dance to the melody of existence that respects the cycles of energy that envelop us.

As we navigate the currents of life, let us strive to embody this dance, moving with grace and fluidity through the myriad phases that define our journey. By doing so, we align ourselves with the cosmic forces that shape our destiny, embracing change as the conductor of our personal symphony, and finding peace in the knowledge that we are an integral part of a larger, magnificent orchestra.

In heeding the call to dance to nature's song, we embark on a path of enlightenment and understanding, one that acknowledges the intricate balance of the universe and our place within it. It is a dance of co-creation with the cosmos, a partnership that weaves the fabric of our lives into the vast tapestry of existence. Through this dance, we discover not only the beauty of the natural world but also the profound depths of our own spirit, learning that in the grand scheme of things, love and trust are our most faithful guides.

In this journey, let us remember that the cycles of life are not mere passages of time but opportunities for growth, learning, and renewal. Let us embrace each phase with gratitude and openness, allowing the universe's wisdom to guide our steps, and finding joy in the realization that, in every moment, we are exactly where we are meant to be. Dancing to nature's song, we find harmony with the universe, and in doing so, we discover the true essence of living.

"The Dance of Life"

Come dance with me now
Don't tell me you won't
Sometimes I'll lead
Then maybe I won't
Let me come close
Hold you so tight
Then move away
You'll know when it's right

Sometimes we'll move fast
Other times slow
Some dances are new
Others we know
Don't let me fall when you Samba with me
Let me fly through the air with the greatest of ease

With a tap on my shoulder
There's someone who's new
He wants to swap partners
Take over from you
Our heads in the air
We do the quick step
He dances so well
For a person just met

Look in my eyes
The past you will see
Your gaze will reflect
The passion in me
This Dance is the one
You move with such Grace
Your hand on my back

Your cheek to my face

The Rhythm of Life
Just go with the flow
Each beat of your heart
Says let it all go
Don't hold it inside
This love of the floor
The dance of your life
Leave them wanting more

I want to sit down
You want to go home
Stay with me now
Don't leave me alone
The night is still young
Let's dance until light
Your hand on my heart
So perfect and right

When you dance with another
In each other you trust
You have hold of their heart
Just love it you must
A dance of your life
Your purpose unfolds
Two souls are entwined
To have and to hold

Blessing *15. Judge Me Not

In a world teeming with judgments—cast from every corner and crevice of our lives—it's Ralph Waldo Emerson's musings that offer a moment of introspection. He writes:

> "The intercourse of society, — its trade, its religion, its friendships, its quarrels,— is one wide, judicial investigation of character. In full court, or in small committee, or confronted face to face, accuser and accused, men offer themselves to be judged. Against their will they exhibit those decisive trifles by which character is read. But who judges? and what? *The Over-soul essay*

This inquiry propels us into a deep dive into the essence of judgment itself, framed by the duality encapsulated in the ancient symbol of yin and yang. This emblem, a harmonious blend of black and white within a circle, serves as a profound reminder of the eternal dance between opposing energies—positive and negative—each seeking equilibrium. It is within this duality that the roots of our judgments lie, sprouting from a soil rich with contrasting perspectives.

Judgment, at its core, is the brain's mechanism of assigning value based on relativity. This assignment is not a mere academic exercise but a deeply ingrained process that shapes our actions and reactions. The gavel of our inner judge does not fall lightly; it is we who often bear the brunt of its harshest decrees. The irony is that the most merciless judge we face is not society or those around us but ourselves. Our inner critic, with its relentless, unforgiving, and often mean-spirited commentary, far surpasses any external adjudication.

But whence comes this penchant for self-judgment? The seeds are sown early, watered by the criticisms of those closest to us and nurtured by the cultural institutions that surround us. From a tender age, we're indoctrinated with messages that whisper of inadequacies and failures, shaping a self-perception marred by judgment. It's a reflection, a mirror that society holds up, not realizing that the image cast back is one of its own making.

Embracing the duality of life's energies offers a path to understanding. Recognizing that "good" and "bad," "right" and "wrong," are merely relative terms, each defined by its opposite, we begin to see life not as a battleground of absolutes but as a spectrum of experiences. This understanding fosters wisdom, a bridge that spans the chasm between opposites, inviting us to view life from a myriad of vantage points.

The antidote to the venom of self-judgment is forgiveness. Forgiving oneself for embracing the unfounded criticisms of youth, for believing in the lies spun by our egos that we are somehow not enough, is the first step toward liberation. This self-forgiveness then extends outward, diminishing the weight of others' judgments to mere shadows of their former selves, irrelevant and powerless.

Our journey through a world of duality is immutable, but our perspective within this dance of contrasts is ours to command. The key to freedom lies not in changing the world but in shifting our perspective. It's a realization that emancipation from judgment is but a thought away, a single leap of faith into the understanding that we are, and always have been, enough.

Ralph Waldo Emerson, with his profound insights into the human condition, beckons us to delve deeper into the realms of self-awareness and understanding. His writings, a treasure trove of wisdom, invite us to reflect on the nature of judgment, both external and internal, and to find within ourselves the courage to break free from its grasp.

In navigating the landscape of self-judgment, we are called to a higher understanding of ourselves and the world around us. It's a call to shed the heavy cloaks of judgment we've donned, to forgive ourselves for the missteps and misconceptions, and to step into a light of self-acceptance and peace. This journey, though fraught with challenges, offers a destination marked by profound freedom and a deep, unwavering sense of self.

As we forge ahead, let us carry with us the lessons gleaned from the dance of duality, the wisdom of Emerson, and the power of forgiveness. May we strive to live in a world where judgments, both of ourselves and of others, are replaced with understanding, compassion, and love. For in the end, it is not the judgments that define us but how we rise above them, how we choose to see ourselves, and how we choose to shape the world with the light of our own truth.

In this endeavor, we are not alone. The journey from judgment to understanding, from darkness to light, is one we share with all who seek a deeper meaning and purpose. Let us then, arm in arm, step forward into a future where we judge not, lest we be judged, and where the only verdict that matters is the one that speaks of love, acceptance, and the infinite potential that lies within each of us.

Blessing *16. Your Time To Shine

As we navigate through the cosmic dance of the ages, the Earth finds herself embarking on a transformative journey towards the Age of Aquarius, heralding a new era known as The Golden Age. This pivotal transition marks a departure from the Age of Pisces, an epoch where the masculine energy, characterized by domination, suppression, and authority, cast a long shadow over the divine feminine, muffling her voice and dimming her light.

Throughout history, women have navigated the turbulent waters of subservience, their luminous essence shrouded by the dense fog of a masculine-dominated paradigm. The societal constructs of this era have systematically suppressed the feminine, relegating her to the margins of powerlessness and silence, denying her the space to embody the fullness of her divine goddess energy.

Within this framework, the soul's journey on Earth, particularly through the vessel of the feminine archetype, has been laden with profound challenges. Women have been endowed with a program of unworthiness, a conditioning so pervasive that it has infiltrated the very core of their being. This program manifests as a propensity for self-sacrifice, a compulsion to prioritize the needs of others to the detriment of one's own well-being. Radiating love outwardly, many women have found themselves depleted, their reservoirs of self-love and self-worth drained by the ceaseless giving of themselves to a world that seldom reciprocates.

This unworthiness program, woven into the fabric of feminine existence, has dictated a narrative of subservience, where women, viewing themselves as undeserving, have shied away from claiming their rightful place in the sunlight, opting instead to support from the shadows, allowing the masculine to bask in the glory that was equally theirs to share.

However, the dawn of The Golden Age signals a seismic shift in this age-old paradigm. As the celestial tides turn towards a harmonious balance between the masculine and feminine energies, the chains of unworthiness that have bound the feminine spirit are being dismantled. This era beckons women to awaken to their true essence, to shed the heavy cloaks of self-sacrifice and to step into the radiance of their divine power.

In this rebirth of the feminine, we witness the emergence of new traits and characteristics that herald the self-empowered woman. She who understands her inherent worthiness, who embraces her right to experience the richness of life's tapestry without apology. This woman is a beacon of authenticity, a vessel of boundless love that begins with a deep, unwavering love for herself. She recognizes that her radiance is not diminished by shining brightly, nor is her strength undermined by vulnerability.

The self-empowered feminine is one of integration, where strength and softness coexist, where wisdom flows from the heart as well as the mind, and where leadership is guided by intuition and empathy. She is a creator, a nurturer, a warrior, and a healer, embodying the multifaceted expressions of the divine goddess within.

As women across the globe heed the call to transcend the program of unworthiness, they are supported by the cosmic energies of transformation and awakening. This process is not merely a personal journey but a collective movement towards redefining the role of the feminine in society, culture, and spirituality. It is a return to balance, where the masculine and feminine energies dance in harmony, each honoring and uplifting the other.

This Golden Age invites all of us, regardless of gender, to participate in the cultivation of a world where the feminine is revered for her wisdom, celebrated for her creativity, and cherished for her essential role in the cycle of life. It challenges us to envision a society where the contributions of women are recognized not as supplementary but as fundamental to the well-being of humanity and the health of our planet.

As we embrace the unfolding of this new era, let us each contribute to the nurturing of the feminine energy within ourselves and within our communities. Let us celebrate the return of the goddess, honoring her with our actions, our art, our words, and our love. In doing so, we not only witness the blossoming of the feminine but also partake in the co-creation of a world that thrives on equity, respect, and mutual support—a world that reflects the true beauty and power of the divine dance between the masculine and feminine.

The Age of Aquarius beckons us forward, into a future where the feminine, once veiled in unworthiness, now stands radiant and sovereign, a testament to the enduring strength and grace of the spirit. In her light, we find a path towards a more compassionate, balanced, and spiritually enriched world, where every soul has the freedom to shine in its authentic splendor.

(To explore this understanding further I highly recommend the book by Jamie Kern Lima, *"Worthy: How to Believe You are Enough and Transform Your Life."*)

Blessing *17. In Search of the Magical Other

At the sublime heart of human relationships, the quest for the Magical Other—a concept eloquently described by James Hollis in *"The Eden Project: In Search of the Magical Other"*—remains a pervasive force shaping our collective imagination and individual aspirations. This archetype of a soulmate, envisioned as the singular entity capable of mending our fractured selves and fulfilling our deepest desires, is a myth that has been romanticized across cultures and epochs, a testament to humanity's eternal search for completeness and unity. Hollis writes:

> "One of the false ideas that drives humankind is the fantasy of the Magical Other, the notion that there is one person out there who is right for us…a soul-mate who will repair the ravages of our personal history; one who will be there for us, who will read our minds, know what we want and meet those deepest needs; a good parent who will protect us from suffering and, if we are lucky, spare us the perilous journey of individuation… Virtually all popular culture is fuelled by…the search for the Magical Other."   p.45

The narrative of finding "the one" who will end our loneliness, understand us without words, and shield us from life's inherent suffering, is a seductive one. It is woven into the fabric of our stories, songs, and cinema, a reflection of our deepest yearnings and fears. However, as Hollis points out, this quest is often a mirage, a projection of our own longing for self-acceptance and wholeness onto another. In the modern landscape of relationships, where the rates of divorce and separation loom large, the myth of the Magical Other reveals its frailty, prompting us to question the very foundations upon which we build our expectations of love and connection.

The disillusionment that arises from the pursuit of this mythical soulmate is not a testament to the futility of love but a profound invitation to embark on a more authentic and spiritually enriching journey—the journey of individuation and self-discovery. The spiritual lessons embedded in the experiences of failed relationships beckon us to confront the uncomfortable truth that another person cannot complete us, nor can they be the sole architects of our happiness or the antidotes to our existential solitude.

This realization, though painful, carries with it the seeds of liberation and growth. It challenges us to turn inward, to reckon with our shadows, heal our wounds, and cultivate a relationship with ourselves that is rooted in self-love, acceptance, and understanding. It encourages us to dismantle the illusions of perfection and completeness that we project onto others and, instead, embrace the complexity and imperfection of our human experience.

In this context, failed relationships transform from markers of personal deficiency to catalysts for personal evolution. They teach us about our patterns, our vulnerabilities, and our strengths, offering invaluable insights into our deepest needs and fears. They remind us that true fulfillment and wholeness are found not in the merging with another but in the courageous encounter with our own souls.

The spiritual path unveiled by the dissolution of the Magical Other myth is one of radical responsibility and empowerment. It invites us to reclaim our agency, to become the authors of our own stories, and to find within ourselves the resources for healing, joy, and connection. It underscores the importance of self-relationship as the foundation upon which healthy, authentic relationships with others can be built.

Furthermore, this journey illuminates the interconnectedness of all life, revealing that our quest for a singular, all-encompassing relationship is a reflection of a deeper longing for unity with the cosmos. It teaches us that the love we seek in the Magical Other is a mirror of the love that permeates the universe, a love that is vast, inclusive, and available to us in every moment.

In the embrace of this universal love, we find the keys to transcending our isolation and loneliness. We learn that completeness is not a state to be achieved through union with another but a realization of our inherent wholeness, a wholeness that encompasses our brokenness, our longing, and our beauty. We discover that true intimacy arises from the courage to be vulnerable, to share our true selves with another, not as halves seeking to become whole but as wholes sharing in the adventure of life.

As we navigate the complexities of human relationships, let us hold space for the pain of disillusionment, recognizing it as a portal to deeper wisdom and connection. Let us honor the relationships that come into our lives, not as final destinations on our journey to fulfillment but as companions on the path of self-discovery. And let us celebrate the love that flows within and around us, a love that is not confined to the romantic ideal of the Magical Other but that dances in the light and shadow of our everyday lives, inviting us to awaken to the beauty of our own souls and the sacredness of all connections.

In this reimagining of our quest for love, we are not diminished by our failures but are enriched by our willingness to learn from them, to grow through them, and to open our hearts to the infinite possibilities of love in its many forms. The myth of the Magical Other, while alluring, ultimately leads us back to ourselves, to the discovery that the love we seek is already within us, waiting to be realized, celebrated, and shared.

"The Book of Life"

As you write on empty pages in the book of life that's yours,
may your story be inspiring, that no one's seen before.
Let your hand be guided by the power of your mind,
a treasure lying, waiting, just for you to come and find.

As you rise with each new morning, that day is yours that waits,
to write upon the page, the story you create.
A poem, an adventure, maybe one of fact or fiction,
see each day before you, let it be your inspiration.

You can write one of love, where he sweeps you off your feet,
two hearts that join as one, true love in every beat.
Turn the page over, the choice is always yours,
does he stay, or does he go, life is like revolving doors.

If I want to have adventure, where I am running free,
I get to choose where and when, on earth I want to be.
I can pack my bags, walk out the door, leave it all behind,
whatever I am seeking, it's waiting there to find.

If you need to write a horror story, that is of your choice.
You can choose a happy ending , where with you they rejoice.
Your story maybe sad, that will make the reader weep.
But even on the darkest pages, there are lessons you will keep.

Do not lose your nerve and give your pen up to another.
For then the book is not your own, it simply is the cover.
The power lies within you, only yours to write and tell.
Keep that pen within your grasp, and it will serve you well.

Never let another tell you what your stories' worth.
For you it will be priceless, a gift treasured from your birth;|

*Leave the readers of your journey, with a book they can't put down,
a story of your life, to inspire and astound.*

Blessing #18. Abracadabra- "I Create as I Speak"

In the grand symphony of the universe, where every star, every whisper of the wind, and every heartbeat contributes to an intricate melody, we find ourselves not as solitary entities, isolated within the confines of our minds, but as integral notes in a cosmic composition. At the very core of our being, beneath the layers of physicality, we exist as energy—vibrant, dynamic, and interconnected with the boundless energy fields that envelop every living creature on this planet. Embracing this truth, that we are inextricably linked to the cosmos and all its inhabitants, heralds the beginning of a transformative journey, reshaping our reality in ways beyond imagination.

With this profound understanding as our foundation, let us delve into the alchemy of words, the conduits of our creative essence. Words, often dismissed as mere vehicles for communication, hold within them the power to shape worlds. They are the vibrations that dance upon the fabric of the universe, weaving tapestries of experience through the emotions and visions they evoke. The realm of advertising and marketing stands testament to the might of words, where the deliberate orchestration of language molds perceptions and reality itself. What was once known as propaganda has now donned the guise of public relations, yet the essence remains unchanged: control the narrative, and you control the experience.

Consider, if you will, a tangible illustration of this principle drawn from the medical practices of the United Kingdom, where health professionals engage new mothers in screenings for postnatal depression. Amongst new immigrants hailing from regions steeped in Punjabi beliefs and culture, this initiative often meets with perplexity. Within their linguistic framework, there exists no equivalent word for *depression* as understood in Western discourse, a phenomenon highlighted in Neel Burton's TED talk, "*The Anatomy of Melancholy.*" This absence of vocabulary begs the question: how can one embody an experience for which there is no linguistic anchor? Moreover, the intensity with which we live our experiences is intricately tied to the words we choose, both personally and culturally. Words possess the capacity to amplify reality, transforming 'serious' into 'catastrophic,' 'hungry' into 'ravenous,' 'immense' for 'big', 'squalid' for 'dirty' … imbuing our existence with a richness of emotion that reverberates through our very cells.

The implications of this linguistic alchemy extend beyond the self, influencing the tapestry of human interaction. Every word we utter, infused with our judgments and opinions, ripples through the collective consciousness, perpetuating cycles of disempowerment and conflict, much like an endless game of Chinese whispers where the original message is lost to distortion.

In the quest for harmony and empowerment, the path forward lies in the impeccability of our words. To be impeccable with our word is to wield the creative force with consciousness, to choose expressions that uplift, inspire, and unite. It is to acknowledge our role as creators, sculptors of reality through the medium of language. This impeccability transcends mere caution; it is an active engagement with the power vested in us, a commitment to use our linguistic gifts to foster growth, understanding, and love.

Miguel Ruiz, in his seminal work "*The Four Agreements*," illuminates the principle of word impeccability, inviting us on a journey of self-discovery and transformation. By embracing this agreement, we step into our power, casting aside the worn narratives of our culture to script new ones, painted with the vibrant hues of positivity and potential. As he encourages: "*Speak with integrity.*"

As we navigate the waters of existence, let us hold fast to the knowledge that our words are the brushstrokes with which we paint our reality. Let us choose them with care, mindful of their impact not only on our lives but on the fabric of the universe itself. In the impeccability of our word lies the key to unlocking a realm of possibilities, where every utterance is an act of creation, every sentence a spell of enchantment that shapes the world anew. It was the ancient Aramaic word "*avra kadavra*" which translates as "*Abracadabra: I create as I speak.*" Words have magic, that's why positive affirmations can be very powerful..

This is not merely a call to action; it is an invitation to step into the fullness of our being, to embrace the creative force within and use it with wisdom, love, and intention. For in the power of our spoken word lies the ability to sculpt our personal reality, to weave a world of harmony, understanding, and boundless beauty—a world where every word spoken is a testament to the magnificent creators we truly are.

Blessing *19. It Ends With You

When embarking on the path of return to our spiritual essence, the journey of the soul is often marked by a profound quest for healing—a journey that seeks to mend the wounds wrought by emotional pain and transform the scars of the past into the wisdom of the present. Among the myriad pathways to healing explored within spiritual literature, the works of luminaries like Louise Hay in *"You Can Heal Your Life"* stand as rays of light, guiding those ensnared in the throes of emotional turmoil towards liberation and self-discovery.

At the heart of many spiritual odysseys lies the challenge of navigating toxic family relationships, those intricate dances of love and pain where the emotional dysfunctions of one generation are unwittingly bequeathed to the next. It is within the family circle of these relationships that our deepest wounds are often forged, and paradoxically, where the keys to our healing reside.

The emotional landscape of our lives is frequently punctuated by triggers, those poignant moments when an interaction with someone close—a parent, sibling, or another family member—touches upon an unhealed wound, eliciting a visceral response that belies the depth of our pain. These triggers, far from being mere irritants, are signposts, guiding us towards areas of our psyche that cry out for attention and healing.

Toxic family dynamics serve as a fertile ground for the proliferation of emotional pain, creating cycles of dysfunction that ripple through generations, making the cultivation of healthy, loving relationships an elusive goal. The inheritance of emotional bruises from our parents, who themselves were marked by their own traumas, becomes a legacy of hurt that shapes our interactions and defines our emotional reality.

In the face of such pain, the instinctive reaction is often to cast the responsibility for our healing onto the very individuals who, in our eyes, are the source of our wounds. We wait, sometimes in vain, for them to lay down the proverbial stick that prods at our tender spots, not recognizing that they, too, are ensnared in their own cycle of hurt, wielding their defences against their own unhealed bruises.

The true path to healing, however, is not found in external alterations but in a profound and often challenging inward journey. It is a journey that begins with awareness, for it is only in recognizing the existence of our wounds that we can begin the process of healing. This inward turn requires us to release the expectation that others must change for our emotional landscape to improve, to understand that the power to heal resides only within us.

As we embark on this quest for emotional intelligence, we delve into the patterns and conditioning forged in the dance of family dynamics, seeking to transform our reactions into responses. This process of "growing up" spiritually is not merely an act of maturation but a profound act of healing that allows us to release ourselves and our loved ones from the chains of past traumas.

The act of healing ourselves spiritually transcends the personal; it is an act that halts the generational transmission of toxic patterns, liberating not just ourselves but paving the way for future generations to live free from the legacy of pain. This is the healing of life itself—a restoration of the soul that enables us to engage with the world and our relationships from a place of wholeness, peace, and profound love.

We are invited to embrace the journey of healing as the cornerstone of our spiritual path, a journey that challenges us to confront our deepest wounds, to seek the lessons hidden within our pain, and to emerge, not unscathed, but beautifully transformed. It is in healing our inner world that we find the key to unlocking a life of deeper meaning, connection, and joy, a life where every encounter, every challenge, and every relationship becomes an opportunity to practice the art of spiritual alchemy, turning the lead of our pain into the gold of wisdom and compassion. Your inner healing and release from the heavy burden of old conditioning and patterns from the past are the greatest gift you can give yourself and life itself. Your legacy will continue to ripple long after you have gone because you boldly declared .. *"It ends here .. with me."*

Blessing *20. The Glory of Friendship

In the intricate tapestry of human connections, friendship emerges as a luminous thread, weaving together souls in a dance of mutual belief, trust, and spiritual companionship. Ralph Waldo Emerson, with his characteristic insight and depth, captures the essence of this bond in asserting that the true glory of friendship transcends the mere acts of kindness and companionship. It resides, instead, in the spiritual inspiration that blossoms when we find ourselves in the presence of another who believes in us unconditionally and entrusts us with the sacred gift of friendship. He writes:

> "The glory of friendship is not the outstretched hand, not the kindly smile, not the joy of companionship, it is the spiritual inspiration that comes to one when you discover that someone else believes in you and is willing to trust you with a friendship."

This spiritual dimension of friendship invites us to explore not just the surface waters of shared interests and experiences, but to dive into the deeper currents of mutual growth, understanding, and support. Within this sacred space, friends act as mirrors, reflecting back to us our inherent strengths and the luminous potential that lies within, often obscured by the trials of life or the shadows of self-doubt.

The commitment to the spiritual growth of another is a profound act of love and faith. It signifies a willingness to walk alongside them on their journey, to hold space for their evolution, and to offer encouragement when the path becomes steep or obscured. Such friendships are not contingent upon the fair weather of life's circumstances but are forged in the crucible of challenge, proving their mettle when the journey takes us through the valleys of hardship or the deserts of despair.

In these moments of trial, the spiritual bond of friendship reveals its true power. It becomes a beacon of hope, a reminder of our inner resilience, and a source of strength that fuels our continued ascent. The knowledge that someone believes in us, even when we struggle to believe in ourselves, can be the key that unlocks the door to our own unexplored chambers of possibility and strength.

Moreover, friendships grounded in a commitment to mutual spiritual growth offer a unique opportunity for transformation. They challenge us to evolve, to shed the layers that no longer serve us, and to step into a more authentic expression of our being. These relationships are characterized by an openness to vulnerability, an exchange of truth, and a shared quest for understanding the mysteries of the soul and the universe.

While some friendships may indeed last a lifetime, providing a constant source of light and companionship, others may be more transient, appearing on our path for a season or a reason. Yet, each friendship, no matter its duration, carries with it a purpose and a gift. Some come to teach us about ourselves, to mirror aspects of our being that require healing or celebration. Others arrive to accompany us through specific chapters of our journey, offering the support or challenge necessary for our growth at that moment.

The ephemerality of certain friendships does not diminish their value; rather, it highlights the dynamic nature of our spiritual journey, where individuals enter and exit our lives as teachers, companions, and catalysts for growth. Each friend leaves an indelible mark on our soul, a fingerprint of love and learning that contributes to the unfolding of our highest selves.

Embracing the spiritual bond of friendship requires an openness to give and receive, to engage in the sacred exchange of trust, belief, and inspiration. It calls for a recognition of the divine spark within each other, honoring that connection as a reflection of the universal spirit that binds all of existence.

As we navigate the vicissitudes of life, let us cherish the friendships that enrich our spiritual journey, acknowledging the profound impact they have on our path. Let us be willing to trust, to believe, and to inspire, knowing that in the sacred space of true friendship, we find a reflection of our deepest selves and a glimpse into the infinite potential that lies within us all.

In this celebration of spiritual companionship, we discover that the journey is not one we undertake alone but in the company of souls who illuminate our path, challenge our growth, and share in the deep joy of our becoming. The glory of friendship, then, is found not just in the moments of laughter and light but in the profound realization that we are seen, believed in, and loved for the essence of who we truly are.

"A Reason, A Season or a Lifetime"

Are you a "reason a season or a lifetime" to that soul you'll one day meet?
Where does your purpose lie to the face you first do greet?
Do you talk, or hug or maybe smile, as you simply pass on by?
Or do you hold their hand in comfort as they sit with you and cry?

For so many different reasons people come into our lives,
At the time when you most need them, like magic they arrive.
When their role is all completed, and your needs have all been met,
They may vanish from your life, and in time you may forget

If you are a person's reason know the power that you hold,
To change a life forever, as their story does unfold.
Be aware of simple gestures that are gifts to those you meet,
Like the blessing of a smile, as you pass them on the street.

If you are a person's season, a different role you'll play.
They will stay a little longer. much more than just one day.
Your friends are those who chose you, because of who you are,
The wisdom that you share with them, make you their guiding star.

Take nothing in return, the pleasure will be yours,
The simple joy of giving, will be your true reward.
The lessons that you share with them, will be ones of your own,
The fruit you bear will be so sweet, from seeds of friendship grown.

As surely as the seasons change, some friendships will dissolve,
There are some things that life will bring, that may not be resolved.
Do not mourn those passing friendships, know it was but for a reason,
Those friends were there for you at times, if only for a season.

For those souls that are your lifetime, who live within your heart,

No time or place can ever, keep your destinies apart.
A union made in heaven, your connection will be deep,
They will bring to you those lessons, a lifetime you will keep.

When you walk into a room, there is Magic all around you,
Inspire the life before you, by the simplest things you do.
Keep those thoughts within your mind, when those Souls you greet today,
Be a "reason, a season or a lifetime," you have a role to play.

Blessing *21. Face Your Fear

In the labyrinth of the modern era, where technology and comforts abound, we find ourselves paradoxically ensnared in a web of fear and insecurity, heightened to a degree unparalleled in history. The ubiquity of mass media, with its relentless bombardment of global calamities streamed directly into the sanctuaries of our homes, has ushered in an age of pervasive anxiety. This constant exposure to perceived threats, this relentless assault on our peace of mind, begs the question: What becomes of the human psyche when it dwells incessantly in the shadow of fear?

The toll on mental health under such unyielding stress is profound. Our bodies and minds, besieged by the specter of perpetual danger, manifest this distress through a spectrum of physical and psychological ailments, from the insidious creep of depression to the ravages of cancer. In an attempt to quell this relentless disquiet, many turn to the ephemeral solace of substances and behaviors, seeking relief in the numbing embrace of addiction. Yet, this escape is but a mirage, offering momentary respite while deepening the chasm of disconnection from our true selves.

This pervasive sense of insecurity not only undermines our relationship with ourselves but casts long shadows over our connections with others. It erects barriers, not of safety, but of isolation, transforming potential bridges of intimacy into fortresses of solitude. Behind the masks we wear, lies a profound vulnerability, perceived as weakness, yet it is through these very cracks that the light of our authenticity struggles to shine.

Society, mirroring the turmoil of its constituents, manifests symptoms of a collective psychosis, leading to an era marked by staggering rates of suicide, depression, and addiction. This crisis of the spirit reveals a profound dissonance between our lived experience and the innate longing for peace, connection, and meaning that defines our essence.

Yet, within this crucible of collective suffering, there lies a beacon of hope, a call to transformation. The very breakdown of the psyche, while harrowing, serves as a clarion call, awakening us to the realization that radical change is not only possible but necessary. This mental and emotional nadir becomes the unlikely soil from which the seeds of a spiritual awakening may sprout.

Fear, then, is not merely an emotion to be avoided or suppressed but a signal, an alert that the constructs of our internal world are misaligned with the deeper truths of our being. It invites us to embark on an inward journey, to confront the shadows that have long governed our lives and to rediscover the luminous core of our existence.

The term psychology, rooted in the ancient understanding of the "psyche" as the soul, hints at this profound journey back to our spiritual essence. It beckons us to explore the vast landscapes of the mind and spirit, to transcend the limitations of fear-based living, and to embrace a vision of life grounded in love, connection, and authenticity.

In the face of overwhelming anxiety and insecurity, we are offered an opportunity for profound growth and transformation. By heeding the call to change, by daring to peel away the layers of fear that have obscured our vision, we can uncover the radiance of our true nature. This process of awakening is not a retreat from the world but a deeper engagement with it, armed with a renewed sense of purpose, clarity, and compassion.

The spiritual awakening catalyzed by our confrontation with fear is a journey of returning to the authentic self, a voyage of discovery that reveals the boundless potential within each of us to craft a life of meaning, joy, and fulfillment. It is an invitation to cast off the chains of conformity, to question the narratives that have shaped our perception, and to courageously chart a course towards a future defined by our highest aspirations.

As we navigate this transformative path, let us hold fast to the knowledge that within every moment of fear lies the potential for liberation, that each challenge is an invitation to expand beyond the confines of our previous understanding, and that within the depths of our being, there exists a wellspring of strength, wisdom, and love, waiting to be unleashed.

In embracing this journey, we not only reclaim our mental and emotional well-being but also step into a more profound alignment with the essence of who we are. We learn to dance with the uncertainties of life, not as adversaries to be vanquished, but as partners in the sacred dance of existence, leading us ever onward towards the realization of our truest, most luminous selves.

Blessing *22.   The Road Less Travelled

In the quietude of reflection, certain films transcend their entertainment value and morph into philosophical odysseys, offering us glimpses into the profundities of life. One such cinematic masterpiece is the 1998 classic, "*The Truman Show*," starring Jim Carey. With each viewing, its layers peel back, revealing a richer tapestry of meaning, particularly for those poised to see beyond the surface.

The film introduces us to Truman, unwittingly the star of his own life-show, meticulously orchestrated by the enigmatic Christof—a name not subtly hinting at a godlike figure, overseeing his creation from a lunar studio. One line, pivotal to the film's philosophy, is Christof's response to why Truman never questioned his reality: "*We accept the reality of the world with which we are presented.*" This statement, simple yet profound, nudges us towards introspection about our own unexamined lives within the confines of a preordained social consciousness.

Society's well-trodden path is paved with collective agreements on what constitutes life's permissible experiences. Venturing beyond this realm invites labels of superstition or irrationality, keeping the extraordinary boxed within the bounds of normalcy. This collective narrative shapes a freeway of life, crowded with travelers, few daring to detour into the unknown, deterred by the inertia of habit.

The concept of the "*hedonic treadmill*" illustrates this phenomenon vividly, depicting life as an endless pursuit of an elusive ideal. Society dangles before us the image of an "*ideal self*," complete with prescribed standards of living, status, and behavior. This projection creates a chasm between this ideal and our present selves, fueling a relentless quest to bridge the gap—a quest that often defines our existence.

Beneath this ceaseless endeavor lies a veil of ignorance, not of concealment but of unexplored potential. Like Truman, we are led to believe in the immutability of our world, unaware that a shift in perception is the first step towards liberation. This realization often strikes in the throes of what is colloquially termed a "mid-life crisis," prompting a reevaluation of life's priorities and the shedding of societal expectations.

The awakening to life's multifaceted paths is a journey from the known to the unknown, from a life defined by fear, conformity, and scarcity to one of boundless potential and freedom. The road less travelled is not hidden but requires the courage to seek it, to question the narratives we've been fed, and to embrace the uncertainty of a life unrestrained by the domes of our constructed realities.

"*The Truman Show*" serves as a metaphor for this existential journey, urging us to examine the fabric of our realities and to dare to envision a life beyond the confines of societal norms. It is a call to break free from the shackles of fear and conformity, to discover the roads untraveled that lead to realms of creativity, adventure, and freedom.

This journey is not without its challenges, for the road less travelled is paved not with assurances but with the promise of discovery and growth. It asks of us to be pioneers of our destiny, to traverse the landscapes of our inner worlds, and to embrace the adventure that lies in the unknown.

As we contemplate the lessons nestled within "The Truman Show," let us ponder the roads we travel, the realities we accept, and the possibilities that lie just beyond the horizon of our courage. May we find the strength to step off the hedonic treadmill, to question the veils of ignorance, and to embark on the journey of a lifetime—a journey that leads us to the very essence of freedom and creativity.

In the spirit of Truman's awakening, may we too seek the paths less travelled, guided by the light of our curiosity and the strength of our spirit. For in the journey of breaking free from the domes of our perceived realities, we discover not just the world anew, but ourselves transformed, ready to embrace the infinite potentials of a life unrestrained.

This road, less travelled by, beckons with the promise of adventure, of self-discovery, and of the untold stories waiting to be lived. It is an invitation to venture beyond the familiar, to liberate ourselves from the narratives that bind us, and to step into the vastness of our true potential. May we have the courage to take that road, to live authentically and fearlessly, in the pursuit of a life that truly reflects the depth and breadth of our spirit.

As we navigate this journey, let us remember that the essence of adventure lies not in the destination but in the journey itself, in the moments of courage, in the acts of defiance against the constraints of conformity, and in the discovery of the myriad paths that unfold before us, each leading to horizons anew. The road less travelled is not just a path of resistance; it is a testament to the resilience of the human spirit, to the unyielding quest for freedom, and to the boundless creativity that lies within each

Blessing *23. The Boldness of Commitment

In the realm of dreams and endeavors, the act of commitment serves as a pivotal force, a catalyst that propels the soul from the realm of potential into the dynamic flow of creation. William Hutchison Murray, in his reflections on the *Scottish Himalayan Expedition* written in 1951, he captures this profound truth with eloquence, drawing attention to the transformative power of definitive commitment. He writes:

> "Until one is committed, there is hesitancy, the chance to draw back, always ineffectiveness. Concerning all acts of initiative and creation, there is one elementary truth the ignorance of which kills countless ideas and splendid plans: that the moment one definitely commits oneself, then providence moves too.
> All sorts of things occur to help one that would never otherwise have occurred. A whole stream of events issues from the decision, raising in one's favour all manner of unforeseen incidents, meetings and material assistance which no man could have dreamed would have come his way. I have learned a deep respect for one of Goethe's couplets: Whatever you can do or dream you can, begin it. Boldness has genius, power and magic in it. Begin it now."

This principle, deeply rooted in the fabric of the universe, reveals that within the act of true commitment, there lies a magic potent enough to marshal the forces of providence in one's favor. Murray's insights echo the timeless wisdom encapsulated in Goethe's couplet, urging us to embark upon our dreams with boldness, for it is within this boldness that genius, power, and magic reside. The journey of bringing an idea to fruition is often fraught with uncertainty and hesitation. Yet, it is in making a resolute commitment that we signal to the universe our readiness to transcend these barriers, to venture beyond the safety of the familiar into the vast expanse of possibility.

Commitment is more than a mere decision; it is an invocation, a declaration of intent that resonates through the cosmos, aligning the energies of the universe with our deepest aspirations. This alignment sets into motion a series of events, connections, and resources, previously obscured by the fog of indecision, now illuminated and accessible on the path to realization. It is as though the universe itself conspires to support the committed heart, weaving together a tapestry of synchronicities that guide and nurture the seed of our vision towards its flowering.

The magic of commitment lies in its ability to transform the abstract into the tangible, to bridge the chasm between the world of ideas and the world of action. It imbues our endeavors with purpose and direction, galvanizing our will and summoning forth the inner resources necessary to navigate the challenges that lie ahead. With commitment, what was once a mere possibility gains substance and momentum, attracting like a magnet the conditions conducive to its manifestation.

This principle of commitment and the subsequent mobilization of providence underscore a fundamental truth of our existence: that we are co-creators with the universe, participants in the ongoing dance of creation. Our dreams and aspirations are not solitary whispers in the void but calls to adventure that resonate with the forces of life itself, inviting collaboration, support, and expansion.

The path of commitment, however, demands of us not only a willingness to act but a surrender to the unknown. It asks that we trust in the wisdom of the universe, in the unseen currents that guide our journey, and in the inherent goodness of the unfolding process. This trust is not passive but active, a dynamic engagement with the present moment, fuelled by the conviction that each step taken in commitment is met with the supportive embrace of the cosmos.

In committing to our dreams, we also commit to ourselves—to our growth, our evolution, and our capacity to transcend our perceived limitations. This commitment becomes a crucible for transformation, a space in which we encounter our fears, our doubts, and our resistance, and are invited to rise above them. It is here, in the heart of commitment, that we discover our resilience, our creativity, and our true power.

The act of committing to an idea or task is, therefore, a sacred act, one that reverberates through the layers of our being and into the fabric of reality. It is a declaration of faith, not only in the viability of our dreams but in our own ability to bring them to life. This faith, backed by the universal energy, becomes the driving force behind a stream of events that conspire to bring our vision into being.

As we stand on the threshold of action, let us remember Murray's words and the promise they hold. Let us step forward with boldness, knowing that in the act of commitment, we unlock the genius, power, and magic within us. Let us begin, and in beginning, let us open ourselves to the infinite support and abundance that await the committed heart. For in this commitment, we not only shape our destiny but become active participants in the grand adventure of creation, co-creating with the universe a reality that reflects the highest aspirations of our souls.

"Who I Met in Heaven"

As I knocked upon the Pearly Gates, I asked to come inside,
The angel stood and stared at me, and gathered at my side.
"What are you doing here? For you it's not yet time,"
"Your purpose yet to be fulfilled, a wondrous life in all its prime."

"My grief was great, the road too hard, I could not take no more,"
"I have no purpose in this life, no reason seem to live for."
The angel smiled and took my hand and said, "Please come with me,"
"Let me show you dear one, the life that you don't see."

In to my mind a vision cast that flashed as memory,
A beggar with his hand held out to seek some coins from me.
Within his cup the cash I placed in answer to his plea,
The beggar's fate now sealed in gold, the Angels let me see.

The street he crossed to buy the food to fill his hunger deep inside,
Within the store a face he knew stood there by his side.
The beggar stared into the eyes of this man that was his son,
The son embraced his father proud and said "Dad, with me please come."

Once again, the Angels cast a second memory.
The rain poured down the river fast, my brother called for help from me.
In I dive to swim to him, a rope tied to a tree,
With gasping breath and aching arms the rope he takes from me.

My brother's life was saved that day to live his fate once more,
For at the age of 24 he was sent to fight the war.
With guns ablaze all around his deeds sought out his heart so brave,
Three wounded men carried in, to be treasured lives he saved.

For a third time the angel shared a scene that was to me unknown.
The scene was one of future cast, the seeds yet to be sown.

"In one day's time you were to meet a soul who's life would join with you,"
"This person you have always loved a soul that you once knew."

"But here you stand, that union lost, your child will not be born."
"So many lives will mourn your loss, their scripts in life now torn."
"Never doubt, but know for sure, each life is purpose driven,
each one with Grace and destiny that God to you has given."

I turn to face my angel and said, "What have I done?"
"My life I need returned to me on the setting of the sun."
The angel took my hand and walked me to the gates,
"Goodbye dear one, take our love, go back and live your fate."

As I awakened from my slumber, my eyes did open wide.
My heart once filled with sadness, now filled with love and pride.
I now know I have a purpose, just like every soul I meet,
It is to fill their hearts with Love, each time that soul I greet.

Blessing *24.   The Game of Life

In the labyrinthine journey of existence, understanding the game of life remains an elusive pursuit for many. David Icke (author, speaker), a figure synonymous with challenging the status quo, posits a compelling notion in one of his presentations: *"If you don't know the rules of the game you're playing, the game will play you."* Without a grasp of the game's rules, we find ourselves unwitting participants, often outmaneuvered by unseen forces and hidden truths. This premise invites a deeper exploration into the nature of reality, urging us to consider the layers of existence that lie beyond the immediate gratification of our senses. The world, as we perceive it, is but the surface of an ocean teeming with depths unexplored and dimensions unseen, obscured from our conscious awareness by the very nature of our sensory engagements.

One pivotal rule that governs the game of life, stark in its simplicity yet profound in its implications, is the ubiquity of deceit. *"Everyone lies,"* a statement that may jolt us with its candidness, resonates with a silent acknowledgment within. We are, by our very essence, social creatures, with a shared communal history where survival hinges not just on the physical but on the social acceptance and integration within the pack. The modern world, with its digital thumbs up and icons of approval, magnifies this ancient imperative, cloaking the primal need for acceptance in the guise of virtual likes and shares.

The utility of the lie, then, emerges as a mechanism of self-preservation, a tool wielded to shape perceptions and navigate the intricate dance of social dynamics. This dance, a delicate balance of give and take, is underpinned by mutual self-interest, often veiled beneath the veneer of ethical living and impeccable conduct. Yet, as history reveals, the potency of the lie scales with its audacity. Adolf Hitler, in *"Mein Kampf,"* elucidates this with chilling clarity, illustrating how the masses, prone to smaller self-deceptions, are paradoxically more susceptible to grander fabrications, too vast for their honest minds to conceive. In 1925 he wrote;

> "In this they proceeded on the sound principle that the magnitude of a lie always contains a certain factor of credibility, since the great masses of the people in the very bottom of their hearts tend to be corrupted rather than consciously and purposely evil ...... and that, therefore, in view of the primitive simplicity of their minds, they more easily fall victim to a big lie than to a little one, since they, themselves lie in little things, but would be ashamed of lies that were too big. Such a falsehood will never enter their heads and they will not be able to believe in the possibility of such monstrous effrontery and infamous misrepresentations in others " (p231)

This insight into the nature of deceit underscores a deeper, more insidious form of lying: self-delusion. The lies we weave for others pale in comparison to the fabrications with which we ensnare ourselves. We yearn for honesty in a world draped in falsehoods, crave authenticity from leaders and institutions that mirror our own dissonance, and seek purity in a landscape mottled with contradiction.

Yet, amidst this mire of deception, the concept of impeccability emerges as a beacon of hope. What does it mean to live with integrity when falsehood seems the currency of survival? The cost of honesty may indeed be steep, threatening the very foundations of our social standing, careers, or financial security. However, the pursuit of truth, of living in alignment with one's inner authenticity, offers a liberation far surpassing the ephemeral gains of deceit.

This courage to embrace honesty, even in the face of potential loss, echoes the sentiments of Mother Teresa in her *"Anyway"* poem:

> "If you are honest and frank, people may cheat you; Be honest and frank anyway.."

It is a clarion call to transcend the game, to redefine the rules not by the standards set by the external world but by the dictates of our own conscience. Understanding the game of life, then, is not merely about mastering its rules but about questioning the very foundation upon which they are built. It invites us to engage with the world not as passive players but as conscious creators, grounded in the frequency of authenticity and truth. In this vibrational reality, what we emit is what we attract, weaving around us a reality reflective of our deepest values and beliefs.

To navigate this game with awareness and intent is to recognize the power of our vibrational existence. It challenges us to be the embodiment of the experiences we seek, to resonate with the frequencies of honesty, integrity, and authenticity. In doing so, we not only transform our personal reality but contribute to the reshaping of the collective consciousness.

The game of life, with its myriad rules and hidden dimensions, becomes a journey of awakening, an odyssey that beckons us to discover the magic of living in harmony with our deepest truth. It is a call to action, a challenge to rise above the illusions and deceptions that shroud our reality, and to step into a space of clarity and light.

In this endeavor, we are guided not by the flickering shadows of falsehood but by the steady glow of our inner light, illuminating the path toward a reality where integrity, love, and truth prevail. As we navigate this journey, let us hold fast to the knowledge that in the authenticity of our being lies the greatest power to change our world, one truth at a time.

Blessing *25.   Winners and Losers

In the dazzling maze of societal norms and conventions, there lies a psychological undercurrent that significantly shapes our perception of life: *loss aversion*. This concept, though rarely discussed openly, is a fundamental bias of human nature, suggesting that the sting of loss is felt more acutely than the joy of gain. This bias underpins a pervasive dichotomy in our culture: the notion of winners and losers, a paradigm that defines our successes and failures, shaping our joys and sorrows in equal measure.

Consider the ubiquitous presence of competition in our lives, from the innocence of childhood sports to the grandeur of the Olympic Games, from reality TV dramas to the realms of academia and professional achievement. This competitive framework posits a singular, coveted position of 'winner', leaving a multitude of 'losers' in its wake. This binary classification, deeply ingrained in our social consciousness, equates losing with failure, casting a shadow over the nuanced spectrum of human experience.

Tennis legend Andre Agassi, in his biography "*Open*", illuminates a profound truth about this dynamic, he writes::

> "But I don't feel that Wimbledon has changed me. I feel, in fact, as if I've been let in on a dirty little secret: winning changes nothing. Now that I've won a slam, I know something that very few people on earth are permitted to know: A win doesn't feel as good as a loss feels bad, and the good feeling doesn't last as long as the bad. Not even close."
> p.167

Agassi's revelation exposes the hollow core at the heart of victory, challenging the notion that success in competition brings lasting fulfillment.

This relentless pursuit of winning, driven by a fear of feeling bad, commands a significant toll on our behavior and emotional well-being, often without our conscious awareness. If the scales are inherently tipped towards more losers than winners in any competitive scenario, it's no wonder that many find themselves grappling with dissatisfaction and, in some cases, profound depression. The transient nature of the neurochemical highs associated with winning—dopamine, serotonin, and others—reveals a cycle of addiction, a relentless chase for a happiness that is, by its very nature, ephemeral.

Society's fixation on competition and the survival of the fittest—a misinterpretation of Darwin's evolutionary insights—fosters a culture of suffering and discontent that transcends personal ambition, fueling conflicts that range from domestic disputes to international warfare. The ramifications of this winners and losers game are far-reaching, impacting not just individuals but the very fabric of our communities and nations.

It's time for a paradigm shift, a reevaluation of the values that guide our perceptions and actions. Imagine a world where experiences are not labeled as wins or losses but appreciated for what they truly are: opportunities for growth, learning, and wisdom. Every moment, every encounter, is a gift, laden with the potential for insight and enlightenment. Albert Einstein once remarked:

> "Everybody is a genius. But if you judge a fish by its ability to climb a tree, it will live its whole life believing that it is stupid."

This insight challenges us to reconsider our criteria for judgment, to recognize the unique contributions and capabilities of each individual. By releasing ourselves from the restrictive labels of winners and losers, we open our hearts to the vast array of talents and potentialities that enrich our world.

This reimagined perspective invites us to celebrate the intrinsic value of every experience, to embrace the diversity of paths that weave through the tapestry of human endeavor. In this expansive view, there are no losers, only participants in the grand adventure of life, each with their own lessons to learn, stories to tell, and wisdom to share.

As we navigate the complexities of our existence, let us choose to define our journeys not by the fleeting highs of victory or the stinging lows of defeat but by the richness of our experiences and the depth of our understanding. Let this be our legacy: a society that values growth, compassion, and the boundless creativity that flourishes when we step beyond the narrow confines of winning and losing.

In the vast, interconnected universe of human experience, we are all contributors to a collective masterpiece, a symphony of voices and visions that together create a harmony richer and more complex than any singular achievement could ever convey. By embracing this holistic view, we discover that we are, indeed, so much more than the sum of our wins and losses. We are creators, explorers, and learners, forever expanding the boundaries of our understanding and the depth of our humanity.

Let us then cast aside the outdated paradigm of winners and losers, stepping boldly into a new era of collaboration, creativity, and collective growth. In this world, every experience is a victory, every lesson a triumph, and every individual a vital thread in the intricate weave of our shared destiny. Together, we can forge a future where success is measured not by the heights we reach alone but by the journey we undertake together, hand in hand, heart to heart, towards a horizon of limitless potential.

Blessing *26. What's Your Motive?

In our ceaseless pursuit of goals, dreams, and milestones, life unfurls a tapestry of experiences, painting a vivid tableau of opportunities and regrets. Yet, beneath the surface of these endeavors lies a profound truth, a driving force that shapes the essence of our journey: motive. It is the engine beneath the hood of our actions, the silent whisper guiding each step, yet its voice remains unheard until we face moments of profound introspection, often at the zenith of our challenges.

The narrative of human endeavor is punctuated by the pursuit of external validations—achievements, accolades, and the ceaseless race towards perceived success. We are like the gazelle, propelled into motion by the lion's chase, living in a state of reactive propulsion, driven by forces outside ourselves. This cycle, while exhilarating, often leaves us chasing mirages, illusions of fulfillment that evaporate upon the slightest touch.

There comes a pivotal moment, a juncture in our lives when the external motivators—the applause, the accolades, the roar of the crowd—dwindle into silence. It is in these quiet, introspective spaces that we confront the essence of our motives. Why do we do what we do? What drives us? Is it the pursuit of wealth, the craving for recognition, or the longing for love and acceptance?

The journey of self-discovery often leads us to the realization that the most profound motivations come from within. The realization that our true desires, our authentic motives, are not tethered to the external rewards but are intrinsic to our being, is both liberating and transformative. It is not the lion outside that compels us to run but the lion within—the indomitable spirit, the inner drive that fuels our passion and purpose.

This introspection reveals the essence of our character, the core of our being, when stripped of the accolades and external validations. It is in these moments of vulnerability, when we feel the weight of the world pressing down, that our true motives shine through. What guides us? What drives us? It is the spirit within, the relentless force that urges us to continue, to push beyond the boundaries of comfort and familiarity, to pursue our path with the heart of a lion.

Discovering our 'why' unveils the motives that propel us forward. It is a journey inward, a quest to uncover the essence that has always resided within us, awaiting recognition. This realization that our true motivations are not dictated by external forces but are born from the depths of our spirit is a profound awakening. It shifts our perspective, changing the way we view success and failure, opportunity and setback.

In this newfound understanding, what once appeared as failure transforms into a stepping stone, an opportunity for growth and learning. The absence of expected outcomes no longer signifies defeat but becomes a canvas for introspection, a mirror reflecting our deepest motives. It is in these moments of clarity that we understand the true meaning of living with purpose, of embracing the journey with the heart and courage of a lion.

The miracle, then, is not found in the external validation or the achievement of goals but in the revelation of our inner motives, the discovery of our 'why.' When this understanding dawns, life unfolds in new, unexpected ways. Doors open, paths clear, and opportunities arise, not because the world around us has changed, but because we have transformed from within. We no longer need the lion to chase us; we become the lion, driven by an inner force, motivated by a purpose that transcends the superficial measures of success and failure.

This journey of self-discovery and the revelation of our true motives is the essence of a life well-lived. It is a testament to the power of introspection, the courage to confront our deepest fears and desires, and the resilience to pursue our path with unwavering determination. In understanding our motives, we unlock the potential to live authentically, to embrace each moment as an opportunity for growth, and to revel in the experience of life with the heart of a lion.

"My Desire"

A fiver the dream of the penny
The mountain the yearning of rock.
The clouds flock to the heavens,
The key delights in the lock.

The night does beg for a new day,
An echo to yearn its return.
A sign points the seeker to tarry this way,
The fire an ember to burn.

Desire is the whisper eternal,
That seeks an endless decree.
Those wishes and dreams so vital,
Are the voice of the soul's inner plea.

Blessing *27. The Spiritual Power of Gratitude

In the vast expanse of spiritual discourse, the concept of gratitude emerges not merely as a practice but as a profound language, a means through which we converse with the universe. This timeless theme, woven into the fabric of spiritual literature, reveals a universal truth recognized by sages and gurus across ages—that gratitude is an act of powerful creation, a declaration of alignment with the abundance and grace that pervades existence. Neale Donald Walsch, in his enlightening dialogue in "*Conversations with God,*" encapsulates this wisdom by asserting that the most potent prayer is not one of supplication but of gratitude. He writes:

> "The correct prayer is therefore never a prayer of supplication, but a prayer of gratitude. When you thank God in advance for that which you choose to experience in your reality, you, in effect, acknowledge that it is there … in effect. Thankfulness is thus the most powerful statement to God; an affirmation that even before you ask, I have answered. Therefore never supplicate. Appreciate." p.11

When looking at life from this perspective it allows us to tune into the universe on its own resonant frequency and gain a more profound comprehension of how gratitude impacts our personal reality.

Walsch's insight illuminates a fundamental shift from seeking to thanking, from asking to appreciating. This shift is not merely semantic but vibrational, signaling to the cosmos our recognition and acceptance of its infinite offerings even before they manifest in our physical realm. Giving thanks in this context is like taking a leap of faith; it shows how much we trust in Divine benevolence and a demonstration of the perfection in our life's unfolding events. The spiritual power of gratitude lies in this ability to transmute our perception of reality

By focusing on what "is"—on the blessings that already inhabit our lives—we align ourselves with a frequency of abundance, opening our hearts and minds to the presence of even greater gifts. This alignment is not a passive acceptance but an active engagement with life, a choice to see the hidden jewels in our trials and the unseen opportunities in our challenges.

The gurus and spiritual masters understood that gratitude bridges the gap between our earthly experiences and our divine nature. It acts as a beacon, attracting experiences, people, and circumstances that resonate with our acknowledgment of life's inherent goodness. By being thankful, we not only recognize the worth of what we have but also open ourselves up to the realization that our prayers are always being answered and our perceived needs are being provided with boundless love and generosity.

This language of gratitude goes beyond words and into the depths of our being, where we understand that we are interdependent and part of something greater than ourselves. It is here, in this space of unity, that gratitude finds its deepest expression, not as a tool for manifesting specific outcomes but as a celebration of the miracle of existence itself.

Gratitude, then, becomes a sacred dialogue, a way of living that continuously communicates our appreciation for the myriad ways the universe supports and nurtures us. It shifts our focus from lack to fullness, from absence to presence, empowering us to create our reality from a place of wholeness rather than want. For little do we realise that as we declare our state of *"wanting"* to the universe it is sending out a message that you are in lack and do not have that what you are seeking. Again, Neale Donald Walsch enlightens the reader on that very proposition:

> "You will not have that which you ask, nor can you have anything you want. This is because your very request is a statement of lack, and your saying you want a thing only works to produce that precise experience – wanting – in your reality." p.11

Alternatively, then, as Walsch points to, the practice of gratitude instead illuminates the path to spiritual awakening, guiding us to discover the divine in the ordinary, the extraordinary in the mundane. It teaches us to find serenity in the simplicity of being, to cherish the fleeting moments of joy and connection, and to acknowledge the profound beauty that lies in the fabric of our daily lives. When this mind set is your predominant way of experiencing your personal reality then you may well find that your spirit is showing you that you never really needed that what you were seeking after all.

Being grateful allows us to see how all life is interdependent. It is from this higher perspective that allows compassion and kindness to blossom in our lives. It fosters a sense of empathy and understanding, reminding us of our shared humanity and our collective journey towards enlightenment. Through gratitude, we recognize the gifts inherent in each encounter, each challenge, and each triumph, seeing them as integral threads in the tapestry of our spiritual evolution.

The spiritual power of gratitude, as revealed by Walsch and echoed through the ages by countless wisdom keepers, is a testament to its transformative potential. It is an affirmation of life's abundance, a declaration of our co-creative partnership with the divine, and a celebration of the eternal now.

As we walk the path of spiritual awakening, let us embrace gratitude as our guiding light, our most heartfelt prayer, and our most profound conversation with the universe. In doing so, we acknowledge the boundless generosity of the cosmos, affirming that even before we ask, we are answered, and in our appreciation, we unlock the doors to a reality where miracles are not the exception but the rule.

Blessing *28. Embracing Transformation

Change, in its myriad forms, stands as the only constant in the theatre of life, arriving either as a guest welcomed with anticipation or as an unexpected visitor at the most inconvenient times. The essence of change, however, is not in its inevitability but in the transformation it beckons from within us. It is a process often marred by discomfort and resistance, yet, for those who dare to embrace it, the journey is replete with invaluable lessons and unforeseen blessings.

Mahatma Gandhi's profound dictum, "*Be the change you wish to see in the world,*" serves as a timeless reminder of the transformative power inherent within each of us. This principle underscores the futility in awaiting external shifts or demanding alterations from others. It is within the crucible of self-evolution that we find the most potent catalyst for change. Such transformation is not just about altering our external reality but about undergoing a profound internal revolution that reshapes our very essence.

Joe Dispenza's book "*Evolve the Brain*" delves into the intricate dance of neurochemistry and change, illuminating why altering entrenched patterns feels so Herculean. Dispenza elucidates the challenge of change as a battle against the neurochemical status quo, maintained by our addiction to familiar emotions and routines. This addiction ensures that our attempts at transformation are met with formidable resistance, manifesting as the insidious voice of procrastination and doubt, urging us to maintain the status quo.

Our spiritual odyssey demands a departure from the well-trodden paths of our habitual behaviors and thoughts, beckoning us towards realms of authenticity, unconditional love, forgiveness, and non-judgment. As we shed the cocoon of our former selves, we not only forge new neural pathways but also unlock the vaults of our latent potential and creativity. This metamorphosis, while inherently challenging, catapults us into a state of being that was once beyond our imagination, marking a profound change from the inside out.

Indeed, the journey of change is arduous, riddled with battles against our inner demons. Yet, it is through these very struggles that we edge closer to uncovering our innermost truths, the uncut diamonds buried within our souls. Charles Darwin, in his contemplation of survival, posited that it is not strength or intelligence that ensures endurance but adaptability to change. This insight from the realm of natural selection transcends its biological roots, offering a poignant metaphor for human resilience and evolution.

To navigate the tumultuous waters of change, we must first anchor ourselves in the willingness to confront and release the old patterns that have defined us. This requires a relentless pursuit of self-awareness, a commitment to excavating the layers of conditioning that obscure our authentic selves. It is a path paved with moments of introspection, courage, and, ultimately, liberation.

As we embark on this journey, it is crucial to recognize that transformation is not a destination but a continuous process of becoming. Each step taken towards internal change is a step towards realizing our infinite capacity for adaptation, growth, and renewal. It is about recognizing that within us lies the power to reshape our lives, to influence our environments, and to contribute to the collective evolution of humanity.

This path of transformation demands a paradigm shift in how we perceive change. Rather than viewing it as a force to be resisted, we must see it as an opportunity to evolve, to expand, and to experience life in its full spectrum. By embracing change as an integral part of our journey, we open ourselves to the endless possibilities that arise from within, allowing our internal shifts to manifest as external realities.

The call to change from the inside out is a call to embrace our true nature as beings of infinite potential. It is an invitation to step into the arena of personal transformation, armed with faith, resilience, and an open heart. As we navigate this path, we discover that the most profound changes are those that begin within, radiating outward to illuminate our lives and the world around us.

In this transformative process, it is essential to cultivate patience, compassion, and a deep understanding that the seeds of change, once planted, require time to germinate, grow, and flourish. We must learn to be gentle with ourselves, recognizing that every moment of discomfort, every challenge faced, is a step towards uncovering our highest selves.

As we journey through the landscape of internal change, let us hold fast to the vision of what we aspire to become, allowing that vision to guide us through the uncertainties and the trials that lie ahead. In doing so, we have the power to not only improve our own lives, but also to become role models for encouraging change for others

In embracing change from the inside out, we align ourselves with the dynamic flow of life, participating fully in the dance of creation and destruction that defines our existence. We become co-creators of our reality, architects of our destiny, and harbingers of a future that reflects the depth of our inner evolution.

Blessing *29. The Secret

In the golden hues of December 2006, amidst the ebb and flow of an ordinary life, a singular CD crossed my path, introducing itself with the unassuming grace of a leaf touching down upon the water's surface. Its title, "*The Secret*," authored by the visionary Australian filmmaker Rhonda Byrne, whispered promises of transformation so profound, they could scarcely be contained within its circular frame. To articulate that this encounter was life-changing would be to dwell in the realm of understatement; it was nothing short of a seismic shift in the fabric of my existence.

The allure of its message was magnetic, potent with the kind of compelling force that beckons one towards the unknown with the promise of discovery—a genie, not confined within the bottle, but rather, extending an invitation to explore realms beyond the seen. "*You can have anything you want...*" it professed, a declaration so bold, so imbued with potential, that it awakened a dormant yearning within me. Compelled, I heeded its call, inscribing my desires into the pages of a journal with a hopeful heart, casting my intentions into the vast expanse of the universe with the faith of a seeker at the threshold of revelation.

The tapestry of my life, woven with threads of anticipation, began to unravel in ways unforeseen, manifesting the fruits of my intentions in a manner that defied expectation. The universe, in its infinite jest, responded to my calls for an enhanced partnership, weight loss, a swimming pool, a new vehicle, and financial abundance, yet cloaked these gifts in the guise of trials—a departing husband, the grip of illness, the transient joy of material possessions, and the fleeting security of financial gain. Indeed, "*The Secret*" had honored its word, albeit through pathways marked by the darkest of shadows.

As the wheel of time spun its course, ushering me seventeen years forward on the journey, a deeper understanding has crystallized within my spirit, illuminating the ancient adage, *"Not getting what you want may be the best thing that ever happened to you."* My odyssey has revealed that the essence of desire, when rooted in the soil of expectation, often sprouts the fruit of disillusionment. Yet, within this apparent discord lies a hidden harmony, a melody of the soul that whispers of a more profound secret, one that the sages and mystics have sung through the ages—not a secret, but rather, a sacred understanding veiled by the illusion of separation.

At the core of our being, where the eternal dance of existence unfolds, there reside but two primal emotions: love and fear. To desire from a place of lack is to waltz with fear, to echo through the universe a refrain of absence. Yet, love, in its boundless generosity, invites us to become the very source of what we seek, to embody the abundance we yearn for in the lives of others. This wisdom, as elucidated by Neale Donald Walsch in "*Conversations with God,*" calls us to a higher purpose, to enact the Golden Rule not as an edict of morality, but as a manifestation of our intrinsic unity. He states:

> "Be the source. Whatever you want to experience in yourself, be the source of it in the lives of others. This is the great secret. This is sacred wisdom. Do unto others as you would have it done unto you."

This revelation, drawing from the deep wells of Buddhist philosophy, unveils the grand paradox at the heart of existence: that by giving, we receive; by loving, we are loved; by healing others, we find our own salvation. The universe operates not in the currency of transactions but in the grace of gifts freely given, inviting us to partake in the divine flow of unconditional love.

Thus, the true secret to happiness, to a life imbued with meaning and joy, lies not in the relentless pursuit of personal gratification but in the simple, profound act of giving. By extending love, kindness, and compassion, we align ourselves with the cosmic rhythm of creation, becoming conduits of the very essence we seek.

As I reflect upon the journey from that pivotal moment in 2006 to the present, I recognize that "*The Secret*" was but the first whisper of a deeper calling—a calling to awaken to the truth of our interconnectedness, to the power of love as the ultimate force of transformation. This journey of discovery, with its trials and revelations, has guided me to the heart of a universal wisdom: that in giving of ourselves, in becoming a source of light and love, we uncover our true purpose and step into alignment with the highest expression of our being.

Now, with the clarity of hindsight and the wisdom of experience, I stand at this juncture in time, a testament to the enduring truth that the greatest gifts often arrive cloaked in the garb of challenges. In embracing the art of giving, in recognizing that every act of love is a thread woven into the fabric of the cosmos, we unlock the door to a life of true fulfillment, a life where every moment is a blessing, not in disguise, but in radiant, glorious revelation.

"Shooting Stars"

You will never see a shooting star when your eyes are looking down,
Hold your head up to the sky, abundant stars you see surround.
Like a promise lying waiting, the brightest lights there'll ever be.
The window of your soul, they call for you to look and see.

Speak to them so softly, in the silence of your mind,
Ask, each and every one of them, for that wish you wait to find.
Each one a special gift, sent from heaven just for you,
Then hold your hand out to receive, that's all you have to do.

What ever you are seeking, it waits to find you first,
Like water in a glass, it's there to quench your thirst.
If you have the faith to cast your fear aside,
A life of sheer abundance, to you it will provide.

Free those shackles from your heart, rid your soul of every hate,
Let their love inside you live, know that is your fate.
Your destiny is yours to claim, it waits so patiently,
With eyes wide open for inspiration, call on it to see.

Know the joy of giving, let the deed from you depart,
Then watch and wait in moments, where each returns back to your heart.
Say thank you every day for those blessings sent to you,
For in gratitude the power lies, for those wishes to come true.

Shimmering stars in darkness, lead you to the morning light.
The way ahead from despair, to faith that burns so bright.
Use the power of forgiveness, God entrusts to you.
For we are only human, mistakes show us that is true.

All you need is to be living, one heartbeat at a time,
The Magic it will find you, it waits there in your mind.

That star you'll be tonight, just look into to the sky,
You Destiny awaits you, on Angel's wings you fly.

Blessing *30.   Entering "The Arena"

I would like to share with you the inspired words of Theodore Roosevelt spoken in 1910 in Paris:

> "It is not the critic who counts; not the man who points out how the strong man stumbles, or where the doer of deeds could have done them better. The credit belongs to the man who is actually in the arena, whose face is marred by dust and sweat and blood; who strives valiantly; who errs, who comes short again and again, because there is no effort without error and shortcoming; but who does actually strive to do the deeds; who knows great enthusiasms, the great devotions; who spends himself in a worthy cause; who at the best knows in the end the triumph of high achievement, and who at the worst, if he fails, at least fails while daring greatly, so that his place shall never be with those cold and timid souls who neither know victory nor defeat."

In the closing chapters of this modest book, a message of profound significance awaits—one that finds its way into your life at a moment ordained by the stars, at a crossroads where the future seems enshrouded in shadows. If this book has journeyed into your hands, it may very well be that you stand on the precipice of transformation, facing adversities that beckon you into *"The Arena"* of your own becoming. This is no ordinary Arena, but a sacred battleground where fear and courage dance in the light of your soul's awakening.

You may find yourself in the throes of uncertainty, watching as the familiar constructs of your existence unravel, thread by thread. Let not your heart be troubled by the specter of fear, for you have entered *"The Arena's"* hallowed grounds where heroes are forged. This moment, daunting though it may seem, is a clarion call to summon the reservoirs of bravery that dwell within you. The spiritual odyssey upon which you embark—a journey often veiled in the darkness of the soul—is a rite of passage that invites the essence of your authentic self to emerge, radiant and unbound.

The process of awakening, of aligning with the profound purpose that has guided you to this incarnation, is underpinned by a universal support that never wanes. In the words of the luminary Von Goethe, *"Boldness has genius, power, and magic in it."* Embrace this boldness; allow the chains of the old to fall away with grace. The doors that close before you do so not as barriers, but as signposts, guiding you toward new horizons that beckon with the promise of renewal. In the art of letting go, in the sanctity of acceptance and the power of forgiveness, lies your liberation from the shackles of resistance.

As you stand in "*The Arena*" of your life's greatest challenges, know that the universe itself bears witness to the valor with which you face the gales of change. The journey to which you have been summoned—a pilgrimage of the soul's unveiling—requires not only time and patience but an unwavering commitment to the truth of your being. Fear not the path that unfolds before you, for in the alchemy of your courage, you will discover that you are invincible.

Remember, as you confront the phantoms of fear that once seemed insurmountable, that they are but illusions, specters without substance. With each step forward, with each act of courage, the shadows will recede, revealing that the tigers which once haunted your dreams possess no real power over you. They are toothless, rendered harmless by the strength of your spirit and the unwavering light of your heart.

This book, a humble companion on your journey, leaves you with a beacon of hope: that within "*The Arena*" of life's trials, amidst the turmoil and the tears, you are being sculpted into the fullest expression of your true self. It is here, in the crucible of transformation, that the greatest gifts are bestowed upon those brave enough to embrace their fears, to stand tall in the face of adversity, and to walk forward with a heart full of courage.

So, as you navigate the sacred journey of awakening, remember that every step taken in *"The Arena"* of your soul's evolution is a testament to the boundless courage that resides within you. You are not alone; you are accompanied by the legions of the brave who have walked this path before you, by the celestial forces that guide your steps, and by the unwavering belief in the magic that unfolds when one dares to confront the darkness with light. Stand firm, dear traveler, for in your hands you hold the pen that writes the story of your victory, a tale of love, resilience, and the indomitable power of the human spirit.

Love and Blessings to you.

Recommended Reading

If it is your desire to expand upon your understanding of the Spiritual journey I recommend the following books:

"The Well: Revealing the Hidden Nature of Reality"
Lilly Andaman

"Maybe the ultimate paradox of life is that from the bended knee of our burdens weighing heavily upon our backs, we will see with greater vision what was before unseen from loftier heights. Perhaps from the valleys of our deepest despair, the journey and path to the mountain of self-discovery is more clearly revealed and seen rising before us. What if seeded within the darkness of emotional turmoil and turbulence, lay hidden a light that would illuminate and shine a path to the inner sanctums of our freedom and truth. For there is no greater shackle on our inherent right to freedom and truth than one imposed by that of ignorance." p.201

"The Kingdom of the Blind: A Discourse in Spiritual Awakening and the Cause of Suffering."
D.L. Lamperd

"A Course in Miracles."
The Foundation for Inner Peace

"Worthy: How to Believe You Are Enough and Transform Your Life"
Jamie Kern Lime

"The Power of Now"
Eckhart Tolle

www.ingramcontent.com/pod-product-compliance
Lightning Source LLC
Chambersburg PA
CBHW071221160426
43196CB00012B/2365